Relentless Mental Toughness and Optimism

Discover How Champion's and Athletes Develop an Unbeatable Mindset, the Old School Grit of Navy SEALs, and Begin to Take Extreme Ownership of Your Life Today

Marcus J. Clark

© Copyright 2019 - All rights reserved.

The content contained within this book may not be reproduced, duplicated or transmitted without direct written permission from the author or the publisher.

Under no circumstances will any blame or legal responsibility be held against the publisher, or author, for any damages, reparation, or monetary loss due to the information contained within this book. Either directly or indirectly.

Legal Notice

This book is copyright protected. This book is only for personal use. You cannot amend, distribute, sell, use, quote or paraphrase any part, or the content within this book, without the consent of the author or publisher.

Disclaimer Notice

Please note the information contained within this document is for educational and entertainment purposes only. All effort has been executed to present accurate, up to date, and reliable, complete information. No warranties of any kind are declared or implied. Readers acknowledge that the author is not engaging in the rendering of legal, financial, medical or professional advice. The content within this book has been derived from various sources. Please consult a licensed professional before attempting any techniques outlined in this book.

By reading this document, the reader agrees that under no circumstances is the author responsible for any losses, direct or indirect, which are incurred as a result of the use of information contained within this document, including, but not limited to, — errors, omissions, or inaccuracies.

Contents

Introduction _____ 1

Chapter 1:
There are Physical Limits but None for the Mind _____ 3

Chapter 2:
Mindset is Everything _____ 11

Chapter 3:
The Mind of a Navy SEAL _____ 21

Chapter 4:
Daily Habits that Strengthen the Mind _____ 30

Chapter 5:
Fragile Mind to Unbeatable Mind _____ 40

Chapter 6:
Must Know the 40% Rule _____ 51

Chapter 7:
Develop the Confidence to Lead _____ 59

Chapter 8:
Techniques from Navy SEALs _____ 68

Chapter 9:
Mental Training of the Top 1% _____ 79

Chapter 10:
How to Actually Break Bad Habits _____ 88

Chapter 11:
The Difference between Winners and Losers _____ 98

Chapter 12:
Guaranteed Strategies to Build Mental Toughness _____ 108

Conclusion _____ 118

Introduction

Experts argue that everyone is born with the ability to develop mental toughness, but that what matters is the drive that they have throughout their lives to be mentally tough. Mental toughness is simply a strong mindset that a person becomes accustomed to and everything they do is embedded in that energy. It is the ability to withstand criticism and to bounce back from setbacks. Others refer to it as the resistance to give in and as the capacity to reach the performance of one's upper aptitude. Essentially, mental toughness can be described as the precursor of behavior that shows an individual's character in action.

Mental toughness is crucial and valuable for every individual at different levels. It forms the basis on which individuals and organizations behave towards situations in life. It is a personality trait which describes mindset. Personality identifies as the specific pattern of thinking, acting, and feeling for individuals. Therefore, mental toughness links mindset and behavior by examining what is in the mind to explain why a person behaves the way they do.

While some people are born and raised to be mentally tough, others learn about its value later in life through their self-awareness journey. It reaches a point in life where one has to learn and understand their systems for them to surge forward and follow a particular path in life. Mental toughness has become popular in the present times due to its relevance in the fields of sports and Navy SEAL training. Lessons from the world's toughest and most successful people are being embraced as everyone's desire to achieve as an individual becomes paramount. Experts agree that the successful people have a lot of attributes in common which contribute to their success, and it is only by emulating the tactics that they use to survive and succeed that everyone else can also succeed.

In this guide, I discuss the importance of mental toughness and how to develop it to become successful from a coaching perspective. The guide also offers insight that is practically applicable in your day to day life.

Chapter 1:
There are Physical Limits but None for the Mind

Mental toughness has been described as a major factor in most of the significant outcomes around the world. It is one of the most used but least understood terms, especially in the sports arena. Mentally tough people deliver more and have a greater commitment to their purpose. This always translates into a top-notch output and timely delivery. Their stress management capabilities help them to remain generally content, and therefore, they are less likely to develop mental health issues. Further, they connect with others easily and handle tough situations tactfully. They are hardly anxious and. They believe that they have the power to control their destiny, and this allows them to remain relatively tolerable to misfortunes. They portray a positive behavior in situations. They are always ready to embrace new opportunities and are always open to learning.

In an era of fast dynamics in the society, therefore, mental toughness is paramount. Leaders, aspiring leaders, or basically success-oriented people, those working in complex and uncertain environments need to be mentally tough. They need to be resilient and ready for the change. We are living in times of great change and uncertainty. It is difficult to spot people in pure pleasure, relaxation, and acquitted refreshment. That "it doesn't matter whether we win or lose" is also too rare a chant in the current times. The world is seemingly highly obsessed about success and the desire to emerge the winner. This applies in all the domains of life including work, education, and sports. Perhaps our drive for success is encompassed by the thought of being the most powerful or intelligent or just being the best. It is a humankind sort of tune to just be at the top or keep improving at the least. As such, usually, the natural mode of selection applies where the fit survives and takes the first position in various lines.

In his book "The Achievement Mindset," Michael Sheard shares insurmountable thought-provoking situations that should be considered by every individual. He poses queries such as "Why some athletes become successful while others fail when faced with misfortunes; how athletes are able to rebound after great failures; what it is that differentiates an athlete who crumbles under pressure from one who thrives through the pressure and overcomes" The answers to these questions, I believe, lie in the successful establishment, implementation, and sustenance of the concept of intellectual strength. The most successful people today realize that it goes far beyond just the basic technicality, but that winning takes on the further dimension referred to as the psychology of winning. The latter integrates a range of varied mental attributes which are often found in intellectual strength skills description.

Relentless Mental Toughness and Optimism

For a long time in history, the concept of mental toughness has been known to be a big cliché in the sporting arena. Recently, however, the field has attracted the attention of researchers and analysts. Therefore, it has become one of the massively-studied fields with researchers aiming at enquiring into the phenomenon and its relevance to other fields, also trying to highlight it since it is one of the least-understood terms in sports. There are numerous texts devoted to conceptualizing and developing this concept of intellectual sturdiness. The increased flow of interest from an interest of the concept into academic fields indicates its prominence among the pioneers; the coaches, sports psychologists, and the athletes themselves. These groups of people progressively recognize that success cannot be based on raw skill alone, but that psychological factors play a core role. In fact, numerous research results link mental toughness to the excellence of performance and term it as a performance enhancer. However, despite the continuous endorsement of this view among vast populations, there is still a section of the somewhat stubborn audience that is reluctant to embrace the seemingly significant philosophy.

Whenever we face any kind of misfortune or find ourselves in difficult situations, it is believed that our performance is mainly influenced by our ability to balance between internal and external demands, i.e., our negative or positive emotional responses to emergent situations determine the impacts such have on us. This calls for the ability to go beyond the pure technical skill or capability and tap into the power that resides within us to optimize situations and enhance performance. Ever too often, we tend to overlook mental fundamentals when faced with situations that require enhanced performance; that which requires us to act promptly and pushes us out of our comfort zones. Generally, the immediate reaction is usually making adjustments to all levels of our physical routine long before the mental aspect of it could even be considered. The next thing you realize is that you could have done better, yet the result is already out. Even in the field of sports, every athletic contest is usually based on the control of the delicate body-mind connection, yet most often, contestants continue to persist on harder physical training at the expense of psychological training.

Yet individuals who turn their focus into the mental training side have an advantage over those who usually cannot do this. The scientific composition of human beings is designed to direct and regulate its existence from the central nervous system, which is the brain. Regardless of the outstanding technical know-how of an individual, the most certain determining factor of failure or success is most appropriately attributed to psychological factors. How well people develop themselves psychologically and how they apply their skills during high-pressure situations is what really counts. The concept of mental toughness is now used to refer to contestants, especially in sports, who possess superior mental attributes, and it is argued that it is the

Relentless Mental Toughness and Optimism

mental game which differentiates performers as good and very good. Simply put, mental toughness will always set you apart where physical and technical skills are held constant. Importantly, however, improving one's mental performance does not by any chance belittle the significant task of improving physical and technical capability. The point that I'm trying to stress is that an individual with what it takes physically through skills and talent can even emerge a better performer if they train mentally. A person who does not possess similar technical capabilities as others they are competing for the same resource and is maybe slightly weaker in this regard may become a better performer if they develop mental toughness and maintain it. The term fitness is used to refer to the desired condition of being able to reach the highest possible level of performance. In the modern day, however, people need to concentrate on reaching a state of optimal mental fitness as well. Talent alone does not amount to success. There are numerous situations whereby highly talented people have experienced energy burnouts due to mental breakdowns and the considerably less talented people succeeded at high levels due to having mental strength.

If you look at today's most job descriptions, you realize that employers are swiftly emphasizing the relevance of having a strong set of soft skills in combination with the hard skills one possesses. In a scenario where two or more candidates possess a similar set of the minimum requirements, the one with success and enthusiastic mindset gets the job. These skills are increasingly relevant for all organizations as they strive to keep ahead of their rivals in their industry. A person with the ability to cope under pressure, to work under minimal supervision, to hit strict deadlines, and to communicate effectively stands a higher chance than the one without such qualities. Strong mental capacity equips one with emotional intelligence, from whence once is able to build strong relationships with others at work, avoid arguments, and be able to handle conflicts from a composed position. Such a person is considered a good employee because despite cases of failure they remain motivated to push on, and even if they come across unreasonable clients, they are sure to handle the situation well by acting like the bigger person. This way they can present an ideal picture of the organization that they work for.

Ideally, there is perhaps no greater thing you can gift yourself than training your mind to be strong and undefeatable. A strong mental capacity brings with it a strong life. You will be able to stand an advantage in any undertaking you engage in. You will be able to be positive because you know regardless of the number of many times life may knock you down you can always collect yourself and move forward. With mental toughness, you will get more much than you lose in life, and you will see failure as an opportunity for you to see better. Mental strength is the element that your opponents fear more than anything. Everyone knows that it is difficult, close to impossible, to defeat someone who never gives up. You decide your future because

Relentless Mental Toughness and Optimism

you know what you've decided to do now. No other person that can decide your fate or fortune for that matter, but you, simply because you can control your mind. Mental strength can be equated to nothing, and that is simply why you will succeed if you set your mind to winning. It does not mean that everything will fall right on your hand for you to use, but because you will make the most out of everything that comes your way. Sometimes, you do not have the energy, and sometimes, everything looks so far out of reach. Sometimes, even others doubt you and your capability. But you should always aim at backing yourself up and show your mental strength. It is mental strength that will determine the direction your life takes after you are tested. Remember that life is a constant learning process, and we learn through mistakes.

The premise of this guide is that if you combine the two types of fitness, technical and mental fitness, you will increase the chances of achieving a top-notch performance every time you indulge in a project or are faced by adversity. You will develop a chance for excellence that would, otherwise, remain untapped and somewhat unattainable. You will be breaking into unique realms of performance enhancement and optimization. Hence establishing and maintaining mental toughness will in the world we live in today determine your success or otherwise a failure. Seek to establish your strengths and weaknesses, so you can improve on your weaknesses every day and use your strengths to conquer every tough condition. Remember that the person who stares back at you in the mirror every time you give it a glance is your greatest obstacle and your greatest strength as well. How well any of these attributes play out is all upon you. The quality of the life you lead is determined by the attribute that you feed most. Feed strength always, and you will be a conqueror always. Feed your obstacle, and you will hardly achieve a thing in your life. Only you can decide what your life is worth.

As a rule of thumb, always remember that the greatest war of all times was not the one fought during the African colonization, neither has that war been fought in the United States or anywhere else in the world. The greatest war is the one fought by your mind. People you meet along the course of your life may always try to dim your hopes and your dreams. It is only the power of your brain that cannot be stopped. Therefore, do not give up! And do not give in!

Chapter 2:
Mindset is Everything

A great author once said that you should feed your mind with success, or it will rot in mediocrity. No one desires mediocrity. The nature of everyone is to move through life with a mission in mind, to govern how they conduct themselves all through in the pursuit of their mission. The path to success is not entirely a path. It is a playfield. You must utilize any chance that comes your way and trample upon anything that brings you down like it was nothing. Most importantly, you have to have a winning mindset. Just like how you approach an interview, one of the most important meetings in one's life, you should approach everything else with a winning mindset.

Some of the failures that you will experience in life are mainly caused by you. While sometimes, luck plays out and you get something in life, you should not approach life from this standpoint. Some people spend their entire life thinking that by luck, they will make it. However, rarely does luck make you succeed without effort. You should believe that you have the ability to conquer in any situation that tests you. Your passion to win must be more than what lies beneath your feet. Any mission that you set out to achieve is accompanied by unreserved defeat. However, you should remember that it is at the moment you are torn down and worn out in the mind that you should take the battle most seriously and fight the hardest.

You are human, and you are bound to reaching a critical point in life. It is at this moment when your success begins to take shape. There are myriads of ways that life can get you down, even though we are operating in our purpose. Our choices take us in one way or another into the battles that we face. Yet, there are numerous ways through which we can set goals and achieve them by focusing on each milestone along the way. Ranging from the entrepreneurs who start up a business from scratch to the student who begins his career pathway back in middle school and refuses to give up on his career dream despite how far it may be and even to the army recruit who begins to undertake a combat training and does not lose sight of completing successfully, we are all warriors in our own grounds. To withstand the never-ending struggles, the most helpful substance is the strength of the spirit that we possess to never yield to pressure.

While we are just too human to endure endless struggle, the truth of the matter is that the body will follow what the mind believes in. Even when we have the drive to achieve our purpose, the battle can be overwhelming. At a given point in time, we will all get to a point where we feel like we are losing our way. Everything we have strived to achieve becomes distant as unpredicted blows knock us down to the sands that we once proudly stood upon. At this point, we should

Relentless Mental Toughness and Optimism

remember the golden rule amongst champions that greatness is not handed down, but it is acquired by those willing to fight for it.

Simply put, feed your mind with success!

Purpose has been emphasized all through by every successful person in whichever field they operate in. Purpose is the first thing that demonstrates that you believe in yourself. It is also the first step that gives the direction and makes you want to excel since it means something to you. Failing to do that, you will give up when the going gets tough. You will ask yourself, for instance, why you are working hard to succeed in a job yet you don't even like it. If it is maybe about meeting your bills only, you could opt to take a loan or your savings to settle the bills. But when it is the passion of achieving something higher than that which drives you, then you won't give up on the job no matter what. Everyone has a set of core values which give them a sense of purpose. For instance, you might have a purpose of putting your abilities to test if you have been rejected way too often. Whatever your purpose is directed toward, let it not be about impressing others. You can rest assured that they are the first ones to laugh at your downfall or when you face adversity. Experts have argued time and over again that intrinsic goals outshine extrinsic goals, i.e., once you do something to fulfill an innate desire, it is easy to grind harder than in other cases.

To establish your purpose, it is imperative that you ponder over the question of, for instance, what you value most in your life and in other people, people that inspire you and what you actually like about them, how you think you are different from others and why most people thank you, what your vision about the future is, and if you are actually moving towards that direction.

Self-Awareness

They say that in every aspect of life, the first step to finding success is always to admit that you have a problem, and then it can lead to the improvement journey-and that has proven to be true. Introspection is the superpower that each of us can employ to analyze positions you have been in in the past so that you can march forward knowing what to pick and what to drop. It is the starting point that leads to massive self-improvement. The ancient Greek philosophy emphasized knowing thyself; a topic that has since then been of great interest to philosophers and psychologists. Research has positioned self-consciousness as a mechanism of self-control. When we focus our attention on us, we compare our behaviors and core values, and we become objective self-evaluators.

Strength is not only about pushing harder. Rather, we need to take a step back from time to time and assess the bigger picture. A former Navy SEAL commander known as Mark Divine argued that self-awareness is your ground to start building the unbeatable mind. Once you know what you are capable of doing and what brings you down, you are much more capable of soaring higher. The best thing about self-awareness is that it equips us with specific techniques to handle situations. For instance, through introspection, you may learn that you are more of a morning person than an evening one. Thus, you decide to make it your do not disturb moment. Even as most successful people would argue, knowledge alone is not enough. You must act on what you have already established. To develop strong self-awareness, start recording a journal, consistently recording your major activities and realizations every day. At some point, say two weeks of recording, find a quiet place, take a deep breath, and reflect about life. This is a great starting point for you to develop an unbeatable mind, being fully aware of yourself.

Goals

All successful people, regardless of their playing fields, attach high significance to picturing themselves as victors in their minds before they actually succeed in reality. They have mastered this significant art and credited it as a core tactic for success. If there is one thing that has been rightfully translated from the sports arena into other domains in life, including business, is the power of visualization. It is exceptionally effective when harnessed and correctly applied. When you set a goal that you want to achieve, it is normal to begin picturing the obstacles that you may face along the way. The problem with most of us is that we often let these obstacles rent space in our head, which inhibits us from moving forward. This is usually the reason why most people are easily content with the ordinary. Do not let this be you. Envision yourself as a victorious person as opposed to letting barriers in your mind hold you back.

Some of the questions you should brainstorm are: What you need to do to achieve the goal, what sacrifices you need to make, and anticipate how you can address any hindrances. Typically, what I mean is that you should ensure your idealized vision shines brighter than anything that may try to make it dull. Most often, picturing yourself as winner increases your chances to win, but without picturing yourself winning you most probably don't win. Spend time thinking about your achievement, understanding as much about it as possible. After setting your goals, allocate sufficient time for each milestone. If you have several doubts, set small goals to motivate you and help you envision yourself as a winner. Achieving various small goals helps build a momentum that you need to get to the big goals.

In Navy SEAL training, for instance, things as small as making your bed in the morning are taken as a significant goal. It offers a sense of pride and sets you for the day ahead.

Team Support
Besides setting goals, you ought to know that nobody can accomplish them alone. We are social beings, and we all need others at various points in our journey. We live as communities, and we find our strength amongst each other. Even as can be borrowed from the

biblical teachings, God divinely places people at various points of our lives to ensure that we fulfill his pre-ordained purpose for us. However, it is upon us to activate and use our destiny helpers to gain the most we can from them.

It is the nature of human beings to establish support in relationships. While it may not always be the case, it is good to find someone who has your back always and is always willing to return the favor. Experts argue that everyone should identify other people who are like-minded and willing to support you. It is always easier to push harder with a team that counts on you and supports you through thick and thin. Most of the successful people have accredited the cultivation and alignment of networks of support. You must have the right mindset, define what you need, and align the right people to your journey.

Preparation

Even with goals and a right team, it all boils down to preparation. As a person set out on a journey for self-fulfillment, you are going to face stumbling blocks along the way. Some things that challenge you will even fall in the category best described as difficult. At such times, it is tempting to jump into action and start doing what you think is good. Chances are that instead of making the situation better, you might actually make it worse. Conversely, stepping back to prepare can make a substantial difference. When we do our preparation really thoroughly, we gain confidence to approach any kind of situation.

Experts agree that the confidence to perform tasks comes from your work ethic. It is as much about preparation as it is about the mindset.

You are the ultimate designer of your own life, and you make the future by visualizing and actually doing things. You have to become conscious of your visualizations so that you can be armed to handle any hurdle that may come your way. Also, to ensure you are well prepared to face the task ahead of you, you can use simulation. This entails practicing the situation in front of an audience who is your support team, which eliminates the fear of uncertainty. When preparing for an interview, for instance, simulating the situation and answering the likely interview questions in front of, say your friends, beforehand, helps you to identify whether your verbal and non-verbal cues are in place and also gives you the confidence to approach the interview.

Self-Talk

When you are out and about hustling and bustling all day long, it is normal to feel low at times. What you need is this: Take a moment and ponder over what you've told yourself today. Was it critical? Was it kind and helpful? How did this inner discussion make you feel?

Ever too often, we tend to worry about what others think about us, but we seldom think about we speak to ourselves. Yet, you have the capability of speaking life or doom to your life. If you are always hard on yourself, you will never have the zeal to focus on your goals. We can all draw from the experience of a Navy SEAL who is under the training bit of controlling breath under water. In a scenario where the oxygen mask is removed from the mouth, an ordinary Navy SEAL would tell themselves that they are going to die, but a strong person would have to say they can handle it. Talking to oneself positively brings change, but negative thinking brings mental torture. Remind yourself that all pain is temporary and that you are going to pull through.

Focus on Progress, Not Perfection

One of the most common things that bring down people is striving for perfection. Wanting to reach the trophy fast but lacking the patience to hone your skills on the path is quite a mistake. We are human, and we are bound to imperfections. It is our different imperfections that make us unique. If perfection is your goal, the outcome will always be a failure. Of course, this does not stop you from setting the bar high. It only reminds you to put your focus on the steps along the way. Incline your mind toward improvement, learning, growth, and understanding.

Once you tie yourself to specific terms, you set yourself up for a win/lose scenario. Conversely, thinking about improvement allows you to measure progress and take pride in it. Although your weakness should not be allowed to occupy the largest bit of your mind, focusing on the weakness is a vital element of your improvement journey. Successful people admit that they spend most of their time focusing on what they have done wrong in the past and debriefing what could have been done better. Most people are torn down by failures, but the strong ones know that failures are teachers that show us what to do next. They present openings that would have otherwise not been realized. Therefore, every time you fail, evaluate to know what went wrong and try to understand how it can be fixed.

Celebrate

Remember that toughness is not all about hard work. You need to take some moments and celebrate even the achievement of minor milestones from time to time. It is such a celebration of the small wins that get you rejuvenated and gives you the strength you need to continue with the journey. Take time to talk and smile with your loved ones out of your busy schedule. This is as important as the hard work that you have. These moments remind us that our struggle is worth every minute.

Furthermore, part of what creates a tough mind is finding happiness in the simplest of things. Experts argue that happiness is a crucial ingredient for boosting our energy. Several pleasurable moments make us happier than a few big moments. Remember that happiness comes from within. Do what you love. Let your mind be taken away by the music. Talk to friends. We are all human beings, and we want to express ourselves creatively. Do this by showing love to others, and never hesitate to dance.

Chapter 3:
The Mind of a Navy SEAL

You have most probably heard of the Navy SEALs, the leading force known for undertaking the most dangerous and secretive missions in the military arena. Most probably, you have also a glimpse of the training that they go through both in the water and on the dry land. The super-elite team that finished the high-profile terrorist Osama Bin Laden in 2011 is still largely covered with enigma. All Special Forces undergo rigorous training, but the Navy SEALs are considered the most highly trained. It identifies among the public as the most elite force and one you can bet on all-around capabilities.

What's more important whatsoever is the mindset that they possess as they undergo training and even in carrying out their missions in real life. Most of the men on mission dedicate a long time of their life to an upcoming fight, making great personal sacrifices. The pinnacle of SEAL training is referred to as the Hell Week, a period of frequent tests in which all who survive possess a common quality. Even when they are under a test of their lives and are in great pain, they manage to think and step out of their pain, face their fears, and consider how they can help a neighbor who may need their help.

Ideally, what they possess is more than a fist of courage and physical capability. Their hearts are large enough to think about the service of others while putting their own lives on the line and dedicate their lives to a higher purpose. Seal Commanders and other experts in the field of life coaching and psychology have advanced the knowledge of how you can think like a Navy SEAL and succeed in any of your life's domains. Your daily routine, they say, should be tied to a goal that you work towards achieving, whether you want to get in shape, to eat right, or start up a business in a competitive industry. Navy SEALS usually train their minds and their physique. With the right tools, the so-called regular person can train to have the mind of a SEAL. All these tools amount to setting appropriate goals and getting to achieve them with ease. One requires elements such as mind control and utmost concentration, emotional resilience, proper visualization, and learning how to rest but not quit.

The following are the rules of thumb that one should have to attain the mind of a Navy SEAL:

Never Procrastinate
Have you ever settled down to complete a significant task, but all of a sudden you discovered you were engrossed in the latest song released in your favorite genre? Or you are checking the latest fashion trend? Or perhaps you suddenly realize that there are emails to be responded to, or your ceiling fan needs dusting even though it is only 10 a.m.? The next thing you realize is that it has already come to the

end of day, and your most significant task is still unfinished. For most of us, procrastination is a strong force that keeps us from completing the most significant and urgent tasks in our lives. It is a potentially dangerous and mysterious force that causes victims to record poor performance at work, fail in school, or even miss out crucial business opportunities.

Experts relate procrastinators with great visionaries who love to fantasize about the great mansion that they will one day have without actually taking the baby steps involved in setting up and building up the house. What they need is to work like the construction workers who lay one brick after the other, consistently and without giving up until the house is built. With potential distractions at an arm's reach in the digital era, it is very easy to find ways of procrastinating. Do not waste any more time making excuses for the things you have to do. We often tend to put off tasks when there is a challenge at hand and find insignificant activities instead. Remember that the easy way out is to rise up to the challenge and handle every day's important tasks.

Also, remember that it is the small things that matter when you put things into perspective about your future. Some projects or simple tasks may seemingly be trivial that they almost do not matter to you. Take it as a rule of the thumb that every little step along the way matters in reaching the big thing you want. This is perhaps the best motivation you can have to cease procrastinating.

Don't Think of Discipline as a Punishment

Forget motivation, you need discipline! Discipline is a popular but narrowly-understood concept. The most successful people have exercised discipline in all their endeavors. It is vital to everyone, and without it, the world around us would be in chaos. It's about discipline to hold on the course by knowing what you are required to do and making it happen. The battlefield is constantly changing. As a seal in a mission, you are getting gunshots from one direction, and at this point, you are expected to lead your team to pursue the enemy in that direction. You require effective communication and flexibility to make that happen. And so is the case in every domain of life! Priorities are going to evolve and shift from time to time. It is about prioritization and execution. While you may not always be motivated to keep working and responding to emerging demands in life promptly, discipline is going to hold you down for any task.

The ability of a person to have self-restricting values allows them to behave in a controlled manner. Discipline gives shape and stability to an individual, and they extend the same quality to everyone and every organization they interact with. The observance of the well-defined and unwritten rules is the basis of success, without which one would choose to do only what makes them happy, avoiding the challenging tasks and ending up unsuccessful.

The 10-Second Rule

Relentless Mental Toughness and Optimism

Impulse decision making is natural to human beings. Some impulse decisions may help to keep you out of pressure, but overall, thinking before you act is important to avoid destroying your chance to achieve your goals. More than often decisions made under the heat of the moment cause detrimental impacts in our lives that we could never imagine.

Failure to pay attention to decisions is the commonest reason people find themselves in dangerous situations. Specialists advise that it is imperative to take a few seconds to assess your surroundings every now and then. Take time to study if there is a questionable activity in an environment you just stepped in, if there are suspicious people, if the place is unusually quiet, if you have an uneasy feeling, if an unexpected person is present, or if anything looks out of place.

Ideally, it takes only about 10 seconds to scope your surroundings and spot danger to avoid it. This is a golden lesson everyone can learn from how the Navy SEALs operate. You'd rather spend the 10 seconds before deciding to act, rather than waste your precious time trying to remedy the aftermath of the poor decision.

Getting to the Top Takes the Right Drive to Do Things the 99 Percent Others Will Not Do

Perhaps one of the greatest quotes that the SEALs have learned to live by is to let go of the life they planned for them to attain the life that awaits them. There is a fine line between having a vision for your life and letting go of the life you have planned. Learn to differentiate the two. Understand that to let go of what you have planned means to get out of your comfort zone. You must be willing to move out of the ordinary living to discover the oasis of wisdom that awaits you at the top. This is the one thing that most of us lack: the drive to be different. To do what others consider impossible. You must dare to be different!

The one thing that you should know is that the 1 percent has a very different outlook on time from 99 percent. They are always aware that time is limited. They also understand that they have 24 hours a day, just like everyone else, but they have to use their time in the most efficient manner. Conversely, the 99 percent believe that time is infinite, and they just use their time carelessly. They imagine that there is still tomorrow, next week, or even next month. The 99 percent value money over time; hence they try to handle everything by themselves to save on money-even the things which they cannot do so well. They end up wasting their time and energy and still do not receive optimal value for the time. Conversely, the 1 percent value time over money; hence they are not afraid to use the money to buy back time. This they do by paying someone for the services such as cleaning that may consume their time. This way they have time to concentrate on what they can do best and what draws them closer to their milestones.

Ideally, the 99 percent trade time for money while the 1 percent trade money for money. Choose the latter group, which believes in partnering and connecting with people appropriate to establish ideas faster, and most importantly, they believe that they do not have to do everything by themselves. Yes, you will seem crazy. Yes, some will mock you. And most definitely, others will only give you a period of time until you can break down. But dare to maintain your focus and never give in to following the multitude. Know that your path is different! Understand that how you spend your time right now determines your achievements tomorrow. The projects you start today will bear fruits tomorrow. What you learn today will be applicable tomorrow. Learn exactly how to value and spend your time as opposed to spend and squander all your time.

Think About the Long-Term

Long-term thinking is perhaps one of the essential skills one can have. Ever too often, you find people planning tomorrow, a few weeks, or months into the future. While there is nothing wrong with such planning, most people do not remember to think long term. Most of the successful people were long-term thinkers who challenged themselves to unimaginably great missions. They chose to plan about the future rather than being confused by the present.

Some of the reasons why long-term thinkers tend to be successful are that they are often willing to make sacrifices that others cannot make. Instead of feeding on life with a big spoon, for instance, a long-term thinking young worker could opt to save up for an investment for when he is older. Long-term thinking parents also begin saving up college fees for their children once they begin toddler classes to avoid amassing huge loans once it's time for college. The point is, become a good long-term thinker, and be ready to make sacrifices today without expecting fruits in a week or a month's time.

Don't Think About Competing Against Others, But Try to Make Progress Yourself

Although life is a competition, it is not a race between you versus others. The real journey of life is the race between you and your unrealized potential. Comparing yourself against others is easy especially in the digital era where they flood our lives with images about their success. There are numerous grounds on which you can compare yourself and against numerous people. This kind of comparison never ends, and you never achieve the real prize of competition. But once you fall for the trap of competing against them, you constantly judge yourself based on their value system. The problem with this is that while you may succeed at it, you only do that which is important for them and not you. At the end of the day, you are still a loser within yourself.

One of the famous mottos that you should all seek to understand is that if any fish compared itself against animals with the ability to climb up a tree, it would forever believe that it is foolish. A SEAL who sets out on a mission to outshine their peers has not succeeded in anything if they do not improve based on their own metrics. Competing only allows you to set goals that fit you best based on what you want to achieve. Comparison against others is always unfair since we presume the best about others and compare it to our worst selves. You are too unique to compete with others fairly. You only have control over your own life and not others. Comparisons take away our joy and add no fulfillment in our lives. Always remember to be aware of your own achievements and unique contributions in this world. Pursue the greater things in life-love, generosity, and empathy- and untie yourself completely from the societal measure of success.

Embrace the Habits Developed Embrace Change

Take it as a general principle that you must create change, or else change will create you. Ever too often, we are resistant to change, and we do not actually realize that change is constant. No matter how much you avoid change, it will, either way, enter your life. A self-initiated change is easier to adapt to since once is ready. Once you realize that you actually have to make certain sacrifices to attain your long-term goals, once you understand that you must be disciplined to succeed, that you should not procrastinate, and that you should make every hour and every minute count, you will have to embrace the change that these success tactics require-and act upon them. Once you sit around and wait to act when the dynamics of life catch you unaware, that is the point at which you make poor decisions, and you cannot control the anxiety that comes with it. To develop an unbeatable mind, you have to be ready to embrace change.

Chapter 4:
Daily Habits that Strengthen the Mind

Unlocking the doors of greatness is not about big gestures. It is much more about taking small steps day by day and being consistent. It is all about pushing a little more every day. To belong to the 1 percent group of people, you must take a deliberate effort to design your life and the habits that you need to develop. One of the greatest philosophers, Aristotle, argued that "we are what we repeatedly do. Excellence then is not an act but a habit." Besides, research has concluded that most of the actions you take every day are not actual decisions but habits. Habits, then, form a way for you to realize your higher purpose. The mindset of the high achievers has always charmed me, simply because of their endless zeal to do what it takes to attain success. They never give up until they are there. And even when they get there, they know that they have to keep up with the habits that led them there, lest they regress. Their failures, their utmost determination in times of difficulties, and the profundity in their priority list is just something to ponder over.

Relentless Mental Toughness and Optimism

We can all replicate these qualities if we learn to understand and control how we live our daily lives. We must, then, develop the habits of successful people.

Do What Most Successful People Do First Thing in the Morning

Wake up early and get out of bed. The manner in which you begin your day plays a central role in how the rest of the day is going to be spent. Feeling your morning with success habits will lead to your progress every day. Therefore, wake up earlier than you have to. Waking up early is no easy task, especially when you are not among the fortunate morning people. Most people do agree that they do not like waking up early. However, successful people always take it upon themselves whether they are morning, evening, or an afternoon individual to plan their mornings the night before and actually wake up early to ensure that they do not miss their schedule. Being an early riser has innumerable paybacks to you as an individual. It has some special power to your mind and body. It gives you time for things such as a healthy breakfast, spiritual and mental wellbeing, proper organization of the day, and a better sleeping routine.

First, when you wake up early before the rest of the world around you, there is a peace and quiet environment for you. Then, you have the time to listen to your thoughts, breathe, and relax. Have this moment to reconnect to your spiritual journey, something that kicks you off for the day. Also, you could listen or read some motivational content and simply sit in silence. Such silent moments in the morning increases your brain's efficiency and boosts your overall health as well. Ideally, you are likely to be more productive when you wake up early.

Remember to Make Your Bed Once You Get Out of It.

While it may look so trivial that you may not attach much meaning to it, making your bed prepares you to go change the world. It is always the little things that matter, and making the bed shows your accomplishment of the first goal. It gives you a sense of achievement and leads you to another task, such as working out since you may not have time for this in any other time of the day. Furthermore, bed-making shows that you can manage the little things, without which you cannot do the big things right. Nonetheless, it feels good to come back home to a well-made bed even if everything did not go well out there.

Create the Ideal Daily Routine

Successful people always establish and stick to their ideal daily schedule. If you are able to start your mornings energetically, that's great! However, to keep being energetic, you must have the right daily schedule. Do not rush into fixing a schedule. Rather, make some few tests to see your most productive time and save that time for the most sensitive task. Ensure that you have time for everything you want to do though. Also, insert breaks within your schedule to breathe and rejuvenate your energy. Use breaks to check on loved ones and confirm your to-do list. This way you are able to multitask without over-pressuring your brain.

Experts argue that structure offers a sense of familiarity; which makes sense only to you. It allows you to wake up with a sense of order and organization. It sticks in you that after a particular task, this comes next. It's even easy this way to create time for an emerging or not so frequent task that you have to carry out on a particular day. Ideally, structuring a daily routine increases efficiency in your life. It becomes a footprint which with or without motivation, feels necessary to follow, and helps you build momentum for getting to your long-term goal.

Your typical day is a successful example when effectively scheduled. In the evening, have some time to unwind, and let go of the stressful moments you experienced at work, and prepare for the next morning. Remind yourself that you did the best and that you can make it. Even if you feel overwhelmed, do not beat yourself up since that's something that all successful people experience. Some days are just too much on you, and you almost feel wasted. Do not let it go to your head. Make peace with everything before getting to bed. You are sure to have a peaceful sleep as you look forward to tomorrow.

Exercise Regularly

Your body is your most important asset; hence it has to be maintained properly. Also, it is true that exercise is food for the body and mind. First, it boosts your energy levels, which is something paramount to a healthy lifestyle. It also helps you to release stress and bring calmness to you.

However, do not fall into the temptation of challenging yourself based on other people's ideal time and ways of working out. Establish what your body needs. One of the most common mistakes that people commit is thinking that they have to go to the gym to lift heavy weights until they pass out. NO! Start out small, and build your pace. Include the habit into your daily routine, and rise up to it. If you are able to have your gym session at exactly the same time, the better for you since you can schedule the activity right before and after that session. Over time, however, try to carry heavy stuff to test your abilities. It is such challenging oneself which builds confidence and the drive of competing against oneself. You will be amazed at how much you are capable of. Also, you will eliminate the fear of what seems impossible for you.

Most importantly, make it a pleasurable moment that you look forward to. Experts argue that your body and mind have to be in sync during your work-out sessions for them to add value to you. If running is not your cup of tea, don't run! Also, try to mix different activities to strengthen different body parts. One of the major benefits associated with this regular exercising is are that it helps to tone and strengthen your muscles. You are able to feel and even look better. It also enhances flexibility, and you are able to carry out tasks without too much straining. It also controls weight and reduce the likelihood of contracting diseases, which could reduce your well-being and productivity. Nonetheless, it improves stamina and helps you to use less energy for the same number of tasks.

Eat Healthy

Food is the fuel that keeps your body going. I agree with the saying "We eat to live, but we don't live to eat." A good diet keeps you energetic to maintain your productivity and keeps you healthy. Every little thing that you consumer matters, whether it is a drink or a meal. Healthy eating is one of the most common concepts but yet which few people practice. Most of us are even unable to differentiate between the great and not-so-great types of meal. It is, however, sad that we do not consider diet as a significant part of our daily habits. You would instantly switch into being more mindful into what you consume if you realized just how a good diet influences your daily energy levels.

Although not all of us are able to eat home-cooked meals, this has proven to be among the easiest hacks into healthy feeding. Most of the restaurants out here are so much likely to add value enhancers such as sugars and flavors to meals. After all, they are in business and their offerings have to be marketable! Cooking at home offers you a chance to control use healthy ingredients and culinary methodologies. One traps that we commonly fall into is the attractiveness of the foods and drinks we find in the supermarkets and fast food stores. It often proves hard to resist the temptation of eating chips, burgers, and sodas when you are out there working and are in a hurry. We find them more convenient, sweeter, and better. However, remember that healthy meals do not have to be every meal that you like. Eat something you do not like but which helps to keep your body healthy.

Healthy eating helps to maintain energy levels and keep you away from sudden sugar crashes or energy burnouts. Staying hydrated, for instance, helps you to stay alert in your work, and you are able to get through each day more easily. It also prevents disease and improves your mental health. Learn to make gradual changes that you can stick to in the long-run. Consider consulting your doctor if you are experiencing problems identifying what food is good and healthy for your body type.

Declutter your Living Spaces and Lifestyles

We live in an era where everything in our lives is in abundance. Due to enhanced production and substitute goods in the market, the cost of goods has decreased, and our living standards have improved in one way or another. Ranging from kitchen stuff, bedroom stuff and clothes, we have everything in higher supply. If you are not keen, you find that you reduce your space by filling it with unimportant stuff. It is essential that you create the habit of eliminating all extra stuff that you do not really need to use. Throw away or give out what you do not need to use.

It is easier said than done. We often feel like decluttering is frustrating, and it's almost like we can't afford a perfectly-organized home.

Relentless Mental Toughness and Optimism

This means to tell you that decluttering should not be difficult. It is enabled when you form the habits that most successful people use to have organized spaces. You should make a plan, and include it in your daily schedule, to take about 15-30 minutes sorting stuff. Do not procrastinate to organize-take it in the same way you would take any other appointment. Ensure that the time you set aside you will have the energy to do so and that you do not have various distractions. Be mindful of what you keep, and start small in your efforts. This helps you feel good about yourself, and it also gives you a sense of pride, which motivates you to keep working on your goal.

Most importantly, understand that decluttering in your life means more than just cleaning and organizing the physical space. Create the habit of eliminating all the life-degrading elements, such as consuming less of social media, toxic relationships, and even the social memberships you never use. This will help you to concentrate on your goal. This is more like applying the 80/2 rule where you identify the 20 valuable things that give you 80 percent of results. Ideally, simplify your life, and only focus on achieving your purpose.

Keep A Journal

Among the best approaches to understanding where you are coming from, where you are now, and where you are headed is to write down your everyday thoughts on various issues. This aids in attaining a proper psychological declutter, compile what you have been learning, improve your visualization about goals and ambitions, and boost your general outlook on life. It is easy to see how much you have grown when you maintain a record of the things you have been doing and setting some time apart every day for that.

To start up, note down one thing you feel you achieved, one thing that let you down and one thing you are grateful about. You will realize that you progress gradually over time and even record other big things, goals, and steps you are taking to achieve. Strive not to skip making an entry twice so you can easily follow up.

Meditate and Carry Out Mind-Focus Exercises

Meditation is among the most profound practices, yet very few practices it. Most of us wonder of what importance it is to just sit or lie there silently, and cannot even draw the line between that and sleeping. Yet, research shows that meditation has immeasurable physical and mental benefits. Similarly, we often ignore the fact that mind-focusing improves our attentiveness to details, among the most crucial skills of decision making. Mind-focus activities access your subconscious mind while meditation accesses your unconscious mind. Also true to this knowledge is that most of the decisions we make are guided by the subconscious mind.

The benefits of meditation include sleep improvement, stress and anxiety reduction, relaxation and energy recharge, anger control, thoughts, and visualization improvement as well as discipline. We cannot ignore the results of such physical and mental boost in our everyday life. Meditation helps us to be at peace with others, focus on the moment, and recharge our energies to continue working. Nonetheless, mind-focusing helps us to not miss important details as we go about our daily lives, and we become more efficient and more successful. Therefore, create the habit of taking some moments to train your mind to focus and to evaluate where you are in life.

Chapter 5:
Fragile Mind to Unbeatable Mind

At the end of the day, mental toughness is what creates champions from amongst us. We are progressively expected to be mentally tough in every domain. We have also been made to believe that tougher is better. Despite that, various factors at play make you doubt your ability to have a thick skin. Your biological composition may be making you more temperamental than others, you may have a degree of depression; you make have had a nasty experience in the past that could include any form of abuse, or, most remarkably, you may not know the necessary coping skills.

A fragile mind is extra sensitive to what is happening around it. Even a slight disturbance that would not because harm can be sensed by the fragile mind. With such a mind, freeing yourself from negative thoughts becomes hard. You always amplify a problem than it actually is. Your mind often spins out of control. You make absurd decisions. However, there is hope for you. You can do better. You can learn how to maintain control over your mind. You can develop an unbeatable mind from a fragile mind. With an unbeatable mind, you don't easily give in, you are fearless, you are strong-willed, and you are emotionally resilient. All you have to do is to embrace the following tactics in your journey toward gaining a thick skin.

You Make Decisions Not Suggestions

Whether your company entails people who wander around looking for a leader or you're amongst a confident lot, you always respond to queries with confidence. You have faith in yourself. Believe it or not, you are constantly portraying your sense of confidence to the people that surround you. This reflects in many ways through your verbal and non-verbal communication. How you say everything matters. Confidence is the cornerstone of everything we do in life, and lack of it has direct implications on our overall achievements in life.

Your mind is snarled up. And getting out of the snarl is proving impossible. But anyway, you have to make a decision. So what? The time is now. Have you made up your mind? Besides, you are generally an indecisive person. Decision making just proves hard for you every time. You always doubt your decisions. Once you make up your mind, you start wondering if it was really the right decision. You just know, or maybe you think, it wasn't the right one. You are just overthinking it, and this is one of the greatest inhibitors of quick and effective decision making.

To develop confidence in what you say and what you decide and also to avoid leaving suggestions for other people to decide about its correctness:

- Refrain from self-analysis paralysis, where you over analyze and spend much time than necessary on something as you try to think what could go wrong and where.

- Understand what a bad decision is, but follow "often a good decision now is better than a great decision later" as a golden rule. This applies especially when it is something you can change later.

- Trust your gut, as successful people have always followed their gut feeling when making the most crucial decisions of their lives. Although thinking accesses the logical part of the brain, if there is a feeling that tells you differently from your mind, consider leaning that way.

You Never are Satisfied with Your Achievements Because You Know You Can Do Better and Want More.

One of the commonest mantras by which the successful people made their accomplishments is moving out of the comfort zone and not settling for less than they believed they deserved. As a success-oriented individual, one of the phrases you never want to settle in your mind is that "this is the way it has always been done." In such a fast-paced society like we are living, even a process you think is really short-lived is already outdated. Therefore, there is most certainly a better way of doing things than it is now. Never rest until your full potential is realized. Try to improve things on your own. Have the mind of an

Relentless Mental Toughness and Optimism

achiever. Just because something works doesn't mean it cannot be made better.

Our human nature tends to make us settle for mediocrity every other day. We tolerate people in our lives even though we dislike them, and we accept jobs that do not serve justice to our skills. We often choose to be complacent while the door for opportunities lies right in front of us. It is always easier to remain in a familiar position than to strive for what is desirable and lies ahead. The major reason why people settle in life is that they fear challenges, change, and taking risks. People create an endless list of excuses to justify their satisfaction with some of their mediocre situations. Such people often end up regretting and wishing they had not settled. Understand that there are always better alternatives out there and you are destined for greatness.

Change your way of thinking, raise the bar, and never accept to settle for mediocrity!

Most importantly, realize that striving to do more while you are never grateful about what you have acquired or achieved now is now worthwhile. There is no point of, say, looking for more money, while you never enjoy it. Being grateful is different from settling. You just appreciate what you already have since growth is part of what makes us happy. A great life always begins with a pleasant mind. Nevertheless, never settle for less than you can be!

Marcus J. Clark

Failure Isn't Recognized Because You Know There's More Than One Way of Doing something.

Failure is an ideology that instills fear and frustration in the minds of so many people. It has a paralyzing effect that tears one down in a rude shock whenever experienced. Thus, it is perceived as a bad thing. However, a tough mind embraces fear like a long-lost friend. Yes, you invest your efforts, your time, and your money only to lose in whatever you set out to do. Yes, you feel bad. It is human nature to love a happy ending in everything, but it is unfortunate that not all results will give you joy. Keep in mind that a baby falls down several times before they can eventually walk comfortably.

You have all probably found ourselves in a position where you begin to blame your fortune and imagine that a particular path is not for us. This is where we go wrong. People with unbeatable minds do not accept failure, because they know there is always another way of doing something. Failure is not actually falling down. But failure is falling down and insisting on staying down while you have a chance to get up. It is the overcoming of failure that creates success. Even the most successful people have failed in so many instances, but they always get up and reach for their success. Nowhere in the world, however, have we heard of a person who achieved anything by giving up. In life as it is in business, any decision that you make leads to two situations, either failure or success. No matter how talented as an individual you are, you do not make every decision rightfully. What matters is what you decide to do after receiving the results. This decision determines what the rest of your course in the path looks like.

In fact, successful people admit that if you do not acknowledge the value of failure, it is hard for you to appreciate the fruits of success. Failure is your best teacher. It improves your focus, keeps you grounded, and helps you realize your better and eventually best potential. Also, failure helps you to inspire others on the verge of giving up. One of the important prerequisites of the success path is staying grounded and heeding the lessons from failure. The most successful businesses in the world did not attain their status overnight. Every big thing had an innovative and risk-taking entrepreneur behind it, one who never gave up and never lost sight of his goal, one who never stopped to admire his work and think he has made it by accumulating wealth. While his ideas failed to deliver at times, he believed that he had the ability to provide consumers with the highest value of the product or service. Then came a global superpower and also came wealth for the entrepreneur.

You Welcome Pressure and Excel In It, You Control Uncontrollable Situations.

Sometimes, life can give you super high stakes, and you can find it difficult to not crack beneath all the pressure. You have too many things to attend to, and you are trying to juggle too many tasks. Experts argue that those with an unbeatable mind are able to thrive under pressure because they approach high-pressure situations in the state of a challenge rather than in the state of a threat. They use their psychological knowhow to enhance their performance in pressuring situations. We should embrace the skills that successful people use to gain a competitive edge in everything. The difference between crumbling and thriving is basically based on how well and fast we analyze the situation to have a quick plan of our response. Responding to such situations as threats always inhibits performance while taking them as challenges in a positive way leads to better performance.

We are all inevitably going to face misfortunes in life. We are human. And that's okay. We respond to these situations psychologically at the trigger of danger. We can either do what the situation demands by enduring the mental responses such as increased sweating or heartbeat or be overwhelmed by the psychological responses. In the latter, our ability to make proper decisions and respond promptly is hindered. Overthinking in pressuring situations can escalate the idea of the situation in your mind; even what you would normally consider manageable becomes difficult for you. Focusing on the task and doing your best is what leads to a reasonable response. Remember that how your body reacts is guided by your mind. Strive to perform optimally and eliminate any thoughts of negativity.

In fact, the pressure you feel is actually in your mind. It takes a moment for you to decide if the situation makes or breaks you. Always

Relentless Mental Toughness and Optimism

adjust the perspective of the moment, eliminate the pressure, and keep your head above the water. Most importantly, stay committed to your goal and rise above the pressure rather than stay passive and let everything overwhelm you. Never lose the sight of your goal even when you feel like things are going down the drain. Maintain your focus toward the lessons such situations bring along and always strive to stay happy.

You're the First One in and the Last One Out. You Work Harder and Longer. After everyone Quits You Keep Going.

Sometimes, especially when you have very challenging goals, you feel like quitting. It is okay to feel that way. However, you should remind yourself to keep working hard no matter what. Do not entertain the feeling of quitting. Persistence in your goals places your winning stakes higher than those of failure. What you should remember whenever you feel like quitting is that you are doing it for a reason. You can even list down your qualities to stop doubting your ability to pull through. There are definitely going to be those times that you got to remind yourself why it's all worth it.

Also, remember that fear is a lie in your head which makes you blow everything out of proportion. Fear is a motivator for strong minds but very destructive for the fragile mind. But fear never has control over you unless you allow it. Remember, also, that you are human and you could need assistance. Never feel afraid to ask for help once in a while, especially during times when you feel overwhelmed. Also, think about how much you are going to regret your decision once everything is back on track and how you will feel horrible for quitting.

Most importantly, remember to always work hard than every other person. Even if it means taking on a path alone, just keep going. What if the rest are focusing on things that are too shallow? Will you follow their manner of working? Remember to aim at establishing yourself as a brand. Branding takes time and hard work. Get strategic, and always focus on your next move. Think ahead and focus on achieving every milestone. Devote time to develop your skills and capabilities. That extra time and energy that others often use for nonissues, you should use for personal growth and expanding your perspective.

You're Humble All the Time Even in Tough Situations

One of the greatest sayings by the poet Tennyson is that humility is the mother of all virtues. Yet the society constantly endorses entitlement, over-confidence, and unending attention on the self. It has increasingly become competitive, making most people obsessed with their appearances and seeking attention. We can all be somewhat prideful at times. After devoting our time and energy into something we tend to develop confidence about it, and it becomes hard to listen to another point of view.

Experts, however, have emphasized the ways in which being humble can improve our psychological well-being. Maintaining a sense of humility exposes you to an oasis of knowledge that expands your intellectually since you are able to contemplate new ideas from different angles. Objectively detach yourself from your knowledge and ability so that your ego does not control you. Humility prevents prejudice of other people since you do not feel entitled to anything. You are able to tolerate others in their own skin, and also you avoid disappointments.

Nonetheless, humble people always know their limits. Hence, they are able to practice higher self-control. You do not block yourself from learning more, and hence you become more knowledgeable day by day. Always maintain the humility to accept that you don't know yet and give yourself a chance to become wiser and greater!

You Are Accountable for All Your Results and Ideas

It might feel like worrying about accountability is a waste of time. You do not even give it time and think about its value. But as successful people would always believe, accountability is what separates the super elite from the mediocre. Whatever gets measured definitely gets managed. The actual thought and effort of carrying out your work from beginning to end are pretty hard-hitting. You find that year after year, you are still spinning the wheels, but you are still facing the same predicament.

One of the major reasons you are not reaching your goals is a lack of accountability. You do not cast blames or point fingers whenever things go wrong in your life. Even though the actions of another may have placed you in a difficult position in your life, refrain from the idea of sitting around just because someone caused you some sort of suffering. Remember, at the end of the day, it is about you and you alone.

Being accountable begins looking in the mirror and accepting who you have become, as you think of the way forward. Accountability keeps you engaged while the road to reaching your goals brings distractions and takes you off-course. It enhances your level of responsibility, and you are able to close all loopholes that may inhibit your chances of success. You will take good care of yourself, and your performance will enhance.

Chapter 6:
Must Know the 40% Rule

The 40 percent rule is a Navy Seals' concept that when we think we are done; it is time we are actually only 40 percent done. It aims at showing us that we have much more ability than we think we do. It helps to explain phenomena such as why almost all the people who start a marathon race actually finish it. Practically, these people are armed with the thought that even when they think it is over, it is actually not over yet.

The 40-percent rule has been applied by the most successful people on their path to goal achievement. They are armed with the idea that they can achieve more than their current achievements. Most of us want to be successful and are willing to do anything, provided it is legal, to achieve success. We often have the energy to start something, anything. But most often, starting is not the problem. Perseverance is what makes us get our prize. All people who achieve and even exceed their expected levels understand that it is often our minds, not our bodies that create obstacles in our path.

The 40-percent rule is a game changer when it comes to triumph. It is an aggressive game plan which shapes you into what you need to achieve what you aspire in the future. The main message that the 40-percent rule sends out is about not giving up when something feels uncomfortable. We often tend to hold ourselves by thinking that we are not capable of. Our insecurities are our greatest enemies. These may have been made profound by the people around us, who may always be pointing them out and criticizing us. For instance, a low performer in the classroom may be criticized and discouraged, especially by the teacher. However, what keeps you in the battle is the purpose that you have.

The 40-percent rule teaches you to rise above your insecurities and the sense of self-doubt. Your insecurities are especially manifest during your time of suffering. You forget that you are great and even you forget all the milestones you have crossed. However, when you focus on the better version of yourself that you want to achieve, you are able to look beyond the perceived limitations. The small things that you do consistently are what results in great things. Little by the little enrolment of habits in your life eventually leads to immense makeovers. Once you are able to start a journey, just know that you can finish it.

Furthermore, in our day to day lives, we often limit the things we can do. We have what we believe we can. For instance, you believe that you can only manage running 200 meters, and if you tried to pass that level, it would not be possible. Do you actually know that the 200 meters in your head are just but 40 percent of the number of meters that you can run? Have you tried to challenge yourself to do more than you do on a daily basis? The 40-percent rule is all about adding small efforts day by day, which keeps adding your percentage. Whenever you think you are tired and that your body or your mind cannot do more-stop to think again.

The great stories of people whose world has at some point have fallen apart and they managed to overcome them can inspire us into applying the 40-percent rule in our lives. Leave alone those who have endured entirely long periods of suffering but eventually pulled through. Think about a marathoner who endures the pain and turmoil in their journey but still makes a point of completing the race. Research has it that 99 percent of people who begin a marathon race in the US normally finishes the race. That is quite surprising considering their struggle to get there.

If we were keen to examine the mind setup of such a marathoner, we would surely draw substantial lessons from their approach of issues. It is obvious that they feel a sense of accomplishment after the race even though they do not try to cover-up how challenging their road to get there normally is. A sports physician once referred to the marathon as a durability event that subjects the body and mind to tremendous stress. During this event, marathoners focus on being present in the moment, and they strive to ignore self-consciousness, which may draw them too much into whatever is going on in their bodies. If they focused their attention on how tired they are or how they have been hit by a hurdle on their way, they might start worrying, and anxiety may inhibit their ability to continue. Most importantly, the power of positivity keeps the marathoners going, since any sense of negativity or defeat may lead to slowing down or dropping out. This way, they are able to realize their full potential of completing the race, more so with minimal injuries. They have mental toughness coping skills that eventually pay off.

Using the marathoners' tips, we can be able to employ the 40-percent rule in our lives: We see that it is the mental focus that helps the marathoners go through a period of about four and a half hours in the zone until they cross the finish line. Believe it or not, you get what you attract. Believe that you can make it and you are already halfway there. Keep doubting yourself, and even the far you have gone in your journey is vanity. While we are used to the idea that to get what we want it has to be hard, we should try to not focus on the ways of reducing the perceived unavoidable suffering. Instead, we should go with the crazy mantra that suffering does not have to be part of the equation. It is really amazing how the whole system works; the things we want to come to us can be achieved with ease and joy. Getting into the space of allowing the law of attraction takes time. We have to shift our energy and start acting in a way that supports our journey rather than hindering it.

Relentless Mental Toughness and Optimism

Give Things a Chance to Be Easy

Whenever we are facing sort of adversity, we try to figure out the best fitting solution. Whenever numerous solutions fail to work, we dig even further with the hope that things will get better. Our minds tell us that we cannot fall back until the solution is achieved. However, the more we dig for the solution, the more we become frustrated and start building a negative momentum. The unpleasant feelings persist in eluding us that we start doubting ourselves and wondering why the universe does not respond to our energy. All this while, however, we are asking for the universe to respond to the wrong energy.

Here's the thing. If you want things to manifest more easily, you must be willing to take a step back, breathe, and let things be. Do not continue down the drain with your frustrations, anxiety, and all the shitty feelings. The time you take to breathe, you align your energy with the road you are taking. Therefore, if you are relentlessly searching for information from the internet, and all of a sudden, you are bombarded with the countless sets of information until you can't tell one from another, get off the internet and use that time to do something else. With your mind lighter, you may be able to come up with a perfect search item that will land you right into what you would have spent hours of searching without bearing fruit. Most often when you step back and relax, something that you have been overlooking along the way will pop up. Your energy is aligned, and you are ready to carry on. Even if you were doing sit-ups, and you thought you are limited to doing 10 times, yet you know you should do at least 50 in a day, take your 5 minutes off, and start all over again. You will find that, with time, you are comfortable doing around 60 sit-ups in a day.

Concede That What You Want Is Not the End

Whatever you think that you want now is only a small fraction of what you are truly capable of. Truth be told, your current desires are based on your vibrations and belief of the current moment. People who lack the energy to continue and quit would grow a little bolder if they knew about the law of attraction. But by and large, most of these things tend to be muted. And that's okay. You don't begin imagining making about 40 grand a month when you are barely striving to get a dime in a month in your new venture.

Our main challenge is being overly attached to particular manifestations in our lives and directing all our energy into this. While the whole idea of stepping back and letting this seems like a good idea, our mind considers it as an enemy to the manifestation of our thoughts. Whilst it makes sense logically to feel connected with what we want to achieve since we can feel its absence, our energy blocks the channels of receiving, through which we can possibly get even better stuff.

The idea here is that you should pay attention to the present and trust that the universe knows exactly what you want. Then, it will be easier to align your energy into achieving more. Just know that when you get your vibe up, you will meet along the way things that make you feel just as good as the pleasant feelings you are currently cultivating. Acknowledge in yourself that what you want is not just what is filling your mind right now. What you truly seek goes much deeper. Most importantly, be willing to concede that you can't even conceive of all the scenarios that would offer you the exact state that you want, and that you would be ready to welcome them if they show up. Just do not be tied by the make-up of your mind that tells you what it feels you should do.

Stop Seeing the Suffering but the Value in It

The society has taught us that to become successful, you have to toil and suffer and work really hard. This is quite unfortunate for the people whose minds begin focusing on the suffering part of their journey the moment they commence it. This paradigm is, in fact, embedded in the minds of many people, especially with all the evidence of people who have achieved great results through suffering and hard work.

It is quite unfortunate to actually believe that hard work and suffering make us worthy of the success we get at the final end. We set our minds to be all manners of miserable for a certain period to get whatever it is that we want. However, we should learn to truly embrace the idea of energetic alignment rather than having pre-determined series of painful endeavors. We should train our minds to accept this and allow things to be easy.

The most disquieting belief that most people possess is that some outside force keeps tabs on all of us and that it will eventually reward us when it decides that our suffering is enough, and it has proven our worth of attaining what we want. After all, we have been made to believe that you must be willing to strain and sacrifice to succeed. With this in mind, the idea that leads our actions is trying to reduce the inevitable suffering, rather than the empowering idea that suffering does not have to be part of the journey. Now start putting things in your mind like what you want may be easy and fun to get there. Think about those activities that give you results with less effort and those which feel good and that to be happy, it is not a must that you pass through a bunch of things that make you unhappy. Start aligning your energy right now to what you can do to make things easier and stop the suffering.

Take it as a general principle that you cannot keep engaging in the suffering waiting to drop them when easier stuff shows up. The universe never defies your vibration. You will actually suffer and lose all your energy when you focus on your suffering. You cannot realize your full potential until you are able to align your mind with what really matters. Things cannot change until you decide in your mind that you will from this point adopt a new perspective to life- that it does not have to be painful and torturous. The energy of allowing things to be will allow you to do more, achieve more, and enjoy the process.

Chapter 7:
Develop the Confidence to Lead

"Be confident" is perhaps one of life's most significant pieces of advice that will make no sense when you've never done something. You already have seen confident people, and you know what they look like, the benefits they reap from being confident, and you also think you would be better with confidence. Most often, we tend to be intimidated by that one confident person who seems to believe in themselves. We tend to look at confidence as a value that one is born with, once we how seemingly flawlessly one presents them. It is easy to even think confident people know exactly how to deal with situations they are engaging with for the first time with ease. But that is usually not the case. For how could they know how it will be before attempting something?

The truth is we are all uncertain about doing something for the first time or taking on a journey, maybe to achieve a long-term goal for a long time. We can all screw up when doing that thing. But whatever it is that differentiates between someone with confidence from one that is not is the attitude. We let our fears and insecurities make us less confident. More so, the mere fact of having never done something that others seem good at makes us think that it as a thing for the lucky few. A confident person does not care how many people have tried down that road and failed and does not listen to noises from the side. They pursue their journey resting on the understanding that they may fail in their experience but also knowing that whatever happens will be alright. Their positive outlook on issues aligns them to their very best mental state to master that situation.

In its simplest form, confidence is the aspect of understanding what you do and the value it adds in whatever field and reflecting this to the audience that may be watching you. There is a thin line between confidence and egotism, whereby the latter can also be referred to as over confidence-and which makes you practically believe that you are better than anybody else hence you start misusing your talent and knowledge to look down on others. Also, there is a sharp contrast between confidence and low self-esteem, whereby the latter makes you think that you are less valuable and cannot achieve things that others do. Imagine that feeling-having the self-approval that you can actually do anything that you set your mind sets out to do. That you actually can stand out amongst a crowd without trying to think that you are better than anyone else.

All confident people were not born like that. They most likely made a deliberate decision to stop fears and insecurities from controlling their lives. They saw the better light of changing the behaviors, thoughts, and even decisions that used to hold them stuck in a cocoon

Relentless Mental Toughness and Optimism

of self-doubt. Things that you can do mentally to start building your confidence:

Being confident is a matter of your mindset. It is just about the way you think. It means having positive thoughts and being confident. Confident people feel a sense of belonging and appreciate others. They often tend to be successful in life because they are confident enough to take on challenges and are always finding positive solutions. Rather than spending their energy on negative thoughts, confident people use their energy to pursue healthy quests.

If possible, healthy confidence building should have taken place earlier on in life-in one's childhood, but a majority of people discover that they should build their confidence levels later on in life in their pursuit of the life they desire. To have the confidence to lead, you have to push through your self-limiting thoughts and beliefs. It is a natural thing to have really huge aspirations as a child, but as you grow up, these aspirations tend to fade off. There are natural inclinations of squashing big dreams. We start letting the society impose on us its own beliefs of our capabilities and weaknesses. To break this off, you have to test your ability by embracing opportunities in life and handling pressure effectively.

Also, develop a sense of curiosity. This will allow you to approach each new experience as fun. Human beings are naturally born explorers, but the confident ones who dare to try new things out become the founders of how we do things. The simplest illustration of how you should treat a new experience is by looking at a playing child. They happily look forward to new involvements because they have not familiarized with the notion of disappointment. To the young child, it is always a chance to learn something new and not a door to disappointment.

Talk to yourself. This is one of the critical mantras that may seem crazy but which actually work. Research has it that we say around up to 1000 words to ourselves every minute. Why not make this count? Talking positively to yourself makes you smarter, improves your memory, and enables you to focus. This is actually one of the aspects that the Navy SEALs are trained on. Speaking positively to themselves helps them overrule fears and deal with anxiety properly. Remember that how you talk to yourself influences the brain's response to it.

In addition, there are tactical actions you should take to improve how you feel about yourself, and consequently what you believe you are worth.

Start by doing what it is that you want to be confident in. Confidence, at the end of the day, is built through experience. Confidence is not an item that you can buy or even borrow. Building it demands action. You have to take solutions every day that will help you start having faith in yourself and being confident. Also, keep doing what you fear, and every step you take brings you closer to what you aspire.

Relentless Mental Toughness and Optimism

Exercise: The benefits of working out cannot be understated when it comes to confidence building. Once you exercise, your body releases endorphins which leave you feeling pretty good about yourself. Also, exercising keeps your body in shape. More importantly, exercising gives you tangible proof that you have done something constructive, and every inch of your body is programmed to endorse that response. If you keep at it and make it your daily habit, exercising results in a healthier body and the results cannot be hidden. It tones you and makes you just look good.

Learn how to dress better: Dressing works magic in how we feel ourselves as we walk and as we interact with others in our day to day activities. Ever looked at yourself in the mirror and gave yourself the first approval before waiting for anyone else to tell you how smart you look? Try that, and you will not be disappointed. One of the common mistakes that we make as humans is that we dress to impress people, and we actually expect compliments while not everyone may actually like your dress code. Once someone points out an error in our dressing code, we become frustrated, and feelings of low self-esteem dominate us. Therefore, we should learn to dress our bodies according to our wishes since we are all unique in our own beautiful way. This way you will not be turned down by any mean comments out there.

Also, realize that how you look is in sync with how your audience views you. More so, confidence is attained by presenting your best self.

Therefore, learn power poses. Our minds can be influenced by what our body is doing. Research has it, for instance, that with outstretched arms, you feel more confident by increasing your testosterone levels. How you position your body directs your mind to feel a particular way, and other thoughts flow from that position. How you carry yourself around also says a lot about yourself to others. Be sure to let them know about your self-confidence and that you are incharge. Learn to walk with your head up and shoulders back since this is the way the world will approach you.

Keep improving your knowledge through research. In an era where almost every piece of knowledge has been brought close to us, we would not have a reason as to why we would take advantage of our devices to improve our know-how. Before you approach someone or something, have a thorough search about it from the internet. A core trap here lies in differentiating between the valid information and the fake since it is all on the internet. Embrace the reading material. Embrace research. E-books are readily available from accredited booksellers and authors. Those, you can be assured, can give you a glimpse of knowledge into whatever field you are seeking. When approaching an interview, for instance, you build your confidence through thorough research about the industry that the company you are interviewing with belongs. You also learn how to behave and respond to questions, and this boosts your confidence and your chances

Relentless Mental Toughness and Optimism

for landing your dream job because you are most likely going to nail the interview and impress your hiring authority.

Below is a checklist of things that confident people do not do:

1. They do not settle for the less than they deserve. While self-limiting thoughts make most people settle for mediocrity, confident people continue to pursue greater challenges and testing their limits even when it feels like they've done too much. They have a vision for what they want and do not let their fears hold them back.

2. They do not look down on others even though they clearly stand out: They do not need to make negative comments about others to build themselves up, something that most of the less confident people do. Instead, they allow themselves to be inspired by successful people.

3. They do not avoid connecting with others. Most often, staying disconnected is a sign of low esteem. You fear to put yourself out there where other people may judge you or even see you fail. The confident people recognize the value of being in a community of people they share ideas and even partnerships.

4. They do not compromise on their values. Having personal guiding principles provides a framework for all that you do in life and

being aligned with these principles ensures you do not compromise yourself based on external or internal pressures.

5. They do not avoid calling out for help when they need it. Lack of self-confidence makes you feel lower when you seek help from others. Confident people, however, understand that seeking help is a sign of strength and not weakness. You develop confidence, and you do not stay there stuck with a problem that you clearly cannot figure out.

6. They do not try changing their personality. They understand that being confident develops from feeling good in your own skin. They also understand that authenticity and uniqueness count in success. They accept themselves and do not compare themselves with others, which is a great thief of self-confidence.

7. They never assume that they are done building their confidence. They understand that confidence requires an enduring vow to rise above feelings of self-doubt. This is because, in everyone's course of life, there are periods of testing one's strength.

8. They do not try to win the approval of others by pleasing them. They never succumb to the need to please people. They go about their lives without the fear of disappointing others when they do not fit their interests. They never compromise on their goals or needs to make others like them.

Relentless Mental Toughness and Optimism

9. Confident people do not let fear hold them back. They understand that fear is a component of success. They focus on heeding the valuable lessons of failure and never take it as an excuse for quitting. Less confident people will quit at the first instance of failure since their low esteem shows them that they did all they could.

Most importantly, confident people believe in winning. They believe in saying YES to opportunities and also saying NO to where appropriate.

Chapter 8:
Techniques from Navy SEALs

It is interesting to learn how the participants in the Olympics handle the pressure of competition when they know they are being watched by the entire world. More so, it is interesting to learn how the Navy SEALs develop the mental toughness to overcome deadly situations. It is also interesting to learn that these two most envied groups of people apply more or less similar tactics in life. Most interesting is to know that the techniques used by Navy SEALs can offer what you need to have an unbeatable mind.

When facing adversities and our lives being threatened, our minds offer us a powerful protection mechanism. It has an automation system which allows us to act before we can come up with conscious decisions. Some of the actions we take during these times may not be the best for us. Navy SEALs are constantly facing life-threatening situations. What keeps them going is the ability to conquer their fear and respond to frightening situations appropriately. They are able to utilize their mindset to make more conscious decisions during these situations.

Relentless Mental Toughness and Optimism

The following is a checklist of the techniques we can all learn from how Navy SEALs build mental toughness.

Setting Goals

Goal setting has been established as one of the most effective techniques that keep you going and focused even when you are facing difficulty, and every inch of your body feels like quitting. It allows you to see the brighter part of the future, and it prevents you from melting down by the heat of the moment. We constantly hear the concept of goal setting, but most often, we connect it to organizations, businesses, or project teams. We imagine that there has to be something big one is aiming. That is where we go wrong.

Goal setting entails all the things, minor and major, that you are looking forward to achieving. You can have a goal for a day, a week, a month or even years. And what do you do after achieving those? You set others. The SEALs are advised to have goals at every single time. Be it in their workouts or working until lunch, they are asked to have something they look forward to achieving. The main thing is to keep improving; hence you must set new goals after achieving the old ones. Be sure to monitor your progress to ensure it aligns with your goal's expectations.

Visualization

Visualization is as important as goal setting. Setting goals is being practical, and visualization is being tactical. It is a strategy you use to anticipate any challenges and get ready to face them. Visualization helps to keep you on your toes since it presents the bigger picture. You see yourself succeeding through all challenges and ultimately accomplishing your goal. The reason we are encouraged to see the bigger picture from both the negative and positive dimensions is that visualizing an ideal situation does not motivate you to put in the required work for you to succeed.

Visualization is a key success factor for the SEALs. Analysis has it that the SEALs spend a considerable portion of their morning time imagining every disaster and error that might occur during the day ahead. This helps them to tie any chance of risk to an appropriate response. They see themselves accomplishing any mission that they are assigned. Typically, by visualizing, you conquer in your mind even before you get to the ground. In every goal that you set, remember to visualize yourself winning so that you are able to ignore critics and eliminate thoughts of self-doubt. You will not have to think about what to do when you are already in a mess. Your mind will guide you on how to stay focused and motivated.

Positive Self-Talk
As mentioned earlier, it is estimated that a person says from 300 to 1000 words to themselves per minute. If there is a comment the SEALs would have to make about this, they would say that those words need to be positive. Tell yourself that you can do it when you give it your best shot. The SEALs always tell themselves this during their

several stressful situations. They look at challenges from a unique perspective and convince themselves that bad things are temporary and that they are going to overcome them. They also say to themselves that all things have a cause, and it is not their fault that things happen the way they do. Their goal is to keep pushing until the end of the tunnel where the light is.

One of the things you need to really realize for your life to change is that every moment is temporary, both good and bad. Your gloomiest moments are momentary. Hence you should not give up on yourself when it is raining in your life. Likewise, the liveliest moments are temporary; hence you've got to live in the moment when the rays of sunshine still warm your heart.

Pessimists do not see anything good when they are in a stressful position. They lose their trust in everyone and everything, and they keep telling themselves that it is their own fault for not having been able to do something correctly. Do not entertain negative self-talk. Kick such ideas out of your head and give space to the positive self-talks that come from an optimistic point of view.

Reciting a Mantra

One of the common habits of the SEALs is forming their own chant that they recite whenever someone tries to show them that they should quit or once the voice in their head is negative. They use this over and over again to condition their brain into thinking that the only option is to keep going. One of the most powerful mantras is that "A man is only beaten in two ways; if he dies off or if he gives up." This conditions their mind into keeping going even if the going gets tough. After all, it is much easier to develop mental toughness when your mind chant is conducive to that development.

Some ideas for mental toughness mantras include that "quitting is not an option," or "Only me can get myself out of the race, and I won't let me."

Simulations

In simple terms, take your visualization and positive thinking to the next level like the experts do it! Simulation entails practically indulging in a situation as close as possible to the real-life situation you are anticipating. Simulations are usually the order of the day during the Navy Seals' training. They try to develop replicas of the situation they are approaching, which helps them shape their training into dealing with what they are to face. They always simulate an upcoming situation and create various conditions they might encounter.

Start acting like the SEALs. Do not sit around and say that when the real time comes, you will rise to face the situation.

How will you manage to stand and deliver a speech in front of a multitude when all you've done is the theoretical part of public speaking skills? To raise your chances of nailing the speech when the actual day comes, try standing in front of small audiences and keep overcoming your fear and correcting mistakes you do while in public. There is a big difference between a person who just does their research to learn the best ways to behave in a situation and one who actually simulates the situation to test it practically.

For instance, a job candidate approaching an interview stands a far much better position when after researching what is expected of them, stands in front of a friend or two who interview them. An interview question, for instance, answered the 50th time is far much better than being said for the first time. Have your friend (s) correct and challenge you from an objective standpoint, so you can identify your strengths and weaknesses and be ready to face the real situation.

Break Down Your Challenge into A Step by Step Process

Breaking down a challenge is compared to the popular chant "eat the elephant." An elephant is considered the biggest animal in the jungle. Eating it literally would take you a long time. But with the goal being finishing eating it at the final end, the only logical step for you to take would be to take one bite at a time. You may not finish it in an hour, a day, a week, or even a month. What is really important is that you are taking a bite after another.

The real secret here is about the breakdown of an intimidating task. The SEALs and the best athletes have always applied this principle to tackle the challenge step by step. They study it to come up with a good way of dissecting it into manageable pieces. Trying to tackle a crucial task all at once may leave loopholes from where the enemy can attack. Basically, the idea is to take your challenge step by step. Set achievable objectives and milestones. As long as you have the desirable deliverables, you are able to tell if the small bite counts towards meeting your standards. Avoid considering the whole as it might confuse and even discourage you.

Focusing on What's Right in Front of You

So, you have broken down your goal or challenge into tiny steps. But then what? It is a huge goal that is probably going to take you long, consuming a lot of your time, effort, and other resources. One of the successful tactics of the SEALs is to first divide a task into tiny steps to keep their mind from wondering how far the finish line is from where they're at, and then to focus on what is right in front of you. Literally put, for instance, a SEAL will most likely focus on crossing the bridge some few miles away, and it is until they cross that that they begin to focus on the next phase.

After all, it is hard to get your mind to actually accept that you have to stay tough for the whole year, but you can easily convince yourself about staying tough for a day.

Raise the Stake:

Commonly referred to as upping the Ante, raising stake means to increase the level of the potential reward of doing something or the risk of not accomplishing it. This determines your level of involvement in a particular situation. When you are actively pursuing a goal, raise the stakes to ensure that you persist until you succeed. You are much more likely to persevere when there is a lot to gain or to lose when you finish a task.

The SEALs have always operated with high stakes, hence the zeal they have for any mission that they undertake. They usually have at stake things such as "If I quit the battle, I will be letting my whole country down," or "If I quit before the mission is over, my family will never respect me again, and I will be setting a bad example to my children." They realize that their individual role counts in the whole group and they stay faithful to their commitment by raising the stakes. Ideally, tricking your mind into believing that there is a lot at stake is likely to keep you going till the end of any mission or journey.

Bouncing Back Quickly After the Unexpected Befalls

To survive the daily life-threatening situations and look forward to the following day with hope and strength, the SEALs are trained to be mentally tough. A vital component of this is a quick come back from the challenge of the unexpected. The SEALs have, therefore, learned not to waste time arguing with themselves on what is actually happening and whose fault it is among the team that there was an unforeseen stumbling block.

For instance, if a team is asked to rescue a person from a situation, they are given the exact outlook of the scene and even the dangerous weapons they might encounter. However, getting to the scene, they might actually find walls that they were not informed about. While a common person, particularly a complainer would start looking for a person to blame or even give up on the mission, the most logical thing that the SEALs take is to acknowledge that it's actually happening, accepting and adapting to it, then acting on it.

Learn to behave and think like the SEALs. You are already in a mess from something unexpected. But so, what? Do not just give up. Focus on how to take on the challenge.

Work Towards Emotional Balance and Control

The benefits of emotional control cannot be understated when it comes to being mentally tough. It is far much easier to focus your mind on relaxing in a stressful situation when you are emotionally stable than when you're not. The SEALs have a simple solution to emotional control. They believe in breathing in for 4 seconds, breathing out for 4 seconds, and doing the same again. Generally, people that are not in proper control of their emotions always get uncontrollably upset when something does not happen as projected. Such people alienate from others, be it friends or family with petty manners.

On the other hand, people who are in control of their emotions are just mentally tough. Hence, they are able to prevent outside circumstances from affecting them. They have developed a thick skin that does not easily crack.

Relentless Mental Toughness and Optimism

You can be sure that there are going to be countless times when things in life will be out of your control. Being emotionally stable gives you the mental toughness to maintain your course with what you had in mind from the beginning.

Identify Where you Belong

The SEALs, though strong individually and whom it all took a personal decision to engage in a mission, work in a group. They work in a community of people they resonate with and who are focused on accomplishing a goal. It is okay to establish your personal goals, but it is also imperative having a team that you resonate with, who shares your interests and ideas, and who have your best interest at heart. The only vital aspect is to draw a line between what is to be shared with others and what should remain personal.

Feeling necessary is food for the soul. It replenishes your energy and keeps you on track. Alone you can walk fast, but together you can go very far. As humans, we crave meaning by associating with others and sharing our values and vision.

Essentially, in every goal that you seek to accomplish, it takes utmost mental toughness to:

- Overcome setbacks and obstacles
- Ignore critics and mean comments

- Remain motivated even when it feels like all hope is gone

- Constantly take appropriate action

- Connect with people you resonate with

- Develop emotional control

Chapter 9:
Mental Training of the Top 1%

As earlier mentioned, the top 1 percent people do not just work hard to get to the top, they must be smart too! If you belong to the 1 percent, you read, listen, and inquire because you are yearning for more from life. You are not like the rest. You are not inclined to taking the easy or path in life or one that feels safe. You know that you can do it, and you actually want to serve as a mirror to people who may be looking up to you. No matter the position you are at in life, there is always a level higher than that. Your treasure awaits you at the peak of the mountain. To get to that level, you must have a relentless self-drive, take the initiative, and refrain from moving with the crowd.

We all know a lot about goals already. Goals are a central reason for the success of the top achievers. They have been the powerhouse behind the building of billion-dollar firms, global superpower inventions, and even why sports superstars have been globally recognized as achievers and received global medals. But it all boils down to how brave you are willing to know your path and stick to it regardless of how the rest of the people behave towards it. It is about the push you have to work hard at all times. Most importantly, it is about the mental capacity that we all need to maintain on our paths and striving to act as an achiever already even though we are not there yet.

We all recognize successful people by their qualities and achievements that set them apart from the rest. We all understand that it is good, and it feels really good to be the best. But what good is that if we do not have the requisite capability and effort to get to that level? There are particular successful thinking habits that often differentiate the top 1 percent from everyone else, the 99 percent others. Research has it that the 99 percent tend to focus their attention on the wrong things, they do not take enough action to fuel their goals, and they prioritize short term comfort over long-term success. Conversely, the top 1 percent people have a mental capacity of managing themselves appropriately and using the resources at their disposal more wisely.

The following are ideas you can use to have the mental capacity of the top 1 percent as opposed to belonging to the 99 percent.

Regularly Review Your Goals

We have already covered so much about setting goals and their role in our life journeys. Now we want to understand why a regular review of goals is paramount for us. The reason why any project, especially in the business field is implemented and followed up with a proper monitoring process is to ensure that everything is moving in the right direction, in what it was intended to. Evaluation is also done to identify the areas that need improvement.

If you are fully committed to your work and taking all appropriate actions, and you feel like your goal is not being achieved, or maybe you have not received results you expected, goal reviewing is what you need. Experts suggest that goals should be reviewed as much as weekly. You may realize that you need a little adjustment to your plans to achieve a particular outcome. It also gives you an honest outlook about your efforts and also inspires you to keep going. Remember it is all about working hard and smart. You don't want to go all the way until you reach your destination and realize that there is a better route that could have gotten you there, with less effort. Also, you don't want to get mediocre results and realize there is something you could have adjusted along the middle of the road and achieved more success.

Identify A Niche Through Which You Can Create Value.

Simply put; focus on being the only one rather than being the best. While the average person thinks about how to become the best in a particular field, a top achiever focuses on identifying the gap in that particular field and creating some unique value. Such a person always looks for ways to complement others who aggressively compete over the same resource by providing them a unique perspective. Articulate what you are good at, and ensure to add value to society. You need not just start competing without knowing what you are really offering.

Sustainable and long-term progress comes from starting out on the right trail. Instead of committing to simply getting ahead and being the best, identify a niche or a 'sweet spot' and pursue that.

Remember to take as a rule of thumb that your uniqueness is what creates value and sells you out. Learn about your strengths, what you are good at and what you are not so good at, and advance from that point. Figure out what works for you and align that with your skill. Develop your own style and follow that.

Attack the Day Very Early in The Morning

We have already covered the benefits of waking up early in the morning. There are various factors that determine whether one is an early riser or late to get to bed. Some of these are variations in lifestyles and natural influences. Yet, it is proven time and over again that the top achievers tend to be very early risers. That one person you probably spot through your window jogging outside while you are struggling to wake up most probably has some secrets to success.

While research shows that evening people are often more creative, our modern society has just naturally inclined to cater to early risers. When the 99 percent others are trying to figure out what to do with their day and fixing tasks, 1 percent of people are already busy into their schedule. There is great enthusiasm brought by waking up early which tunes you into the day ahead. Early risers make the most of the early hours.

Complement Your Knowledge with Action

All other success factors held constant, the top 1 percent of people realize that every piece of knowledge should be followed by a plan that is persistently and aggressively pursued. One of the benefits of taking actions and practically testing your knowledge is that you obtain more control over your journey's direction. You get a chance to advance your skills, experience, and qualifications.

Remember that experience is the best teacher. You are your own driver, and you ought to realize that you should be the mastermind of change. Also, remember that you become unique by being creative to come up with a unique selling point. You attain this level by actually testing your knowledge. Merge your talent and skills to make yourself more marketable. We all need something extra for us to be unique in the information-driven society where everyone has unlimited access to information.

Create Your System

Be assured that the top 1 percent looks for systems to implement. They put the right systems in place, and this sets them to the path of achieving goals. Just as Simon Sinek would say, "Imagine a system where everyone would wake up every day motivated to get to work and finish the day feeling complete by the work they've done, feeling that they have contributed to something better than themselves. The top achievers mostly wake up ready to share everything they have with the world because they realize that it is so aligned with what they care about. It takes a little bit of retrospection to develop your own system.

Identify what is important to you, the times that you are the happiest and even if not for the money, how you would spend your every day. Create and implement a healthy feeding and exercising scheme to achieve mental health and fitness.

Have Priorities

The experts agree that having too many primaries is similar to having none. You cannot be a teacher, artist, yoga expert, and a house painter. Be articulate enough to cut down your priorities and remain with the ones that really matter to you.

The concept of prioritizing is by far and large the reason why some people are always moving but getting nowhere; it is the reason why most people may not be as successful as they may want to be. Most often, such people do not clearly define their priorities. Hence, they lack have motivation. Priorities define a person and give one the reason to do stuff. Prioritizing on one area that you deem best allows you to focus your energy and incline into winning and not giving up. It allows you to measure how good you are at something and it determines where you focus most of your energy and resources. Hence, while most people try to tackle too many things at once, be like the top 1 percent achievers who are pros at prioritizing.

Network

Relentless Mental Toughness and Optimism

No such thing as too many friends. The more people you know, the more connections you have and definitely the more chances of acquiring knowledge and opportunities. The top 1 percent achievers consider networking a necessity in their journey. More so, knowing the right people is a powerful tool for reaching the top 1 percent.

Most people shy away from the thought of having to grow the number of people they know. Yet networking is one of the greatest pieces of advice you'll find in the professional environment. Factors such as educational achievement, experience, and skills held constant, a job seeker who has connections is much more likely to land a job easier and quicker than one who does not. Networking applies in our personal lives. Ideally, the more people we know that are right, the easier it is to achieve something.

The top 1 percent achievers stand out by excelling at networking, informs people how they are doing in life in an intriguing manner. If someone is new to them, they offer some additional information which makes their first encounter memorable.

Comprehend Your Flaws and Specialties
The top 1 percent achievers understand and differentiate between what they can do and what they cannot do. They utilize their strengths to cover up for their weaknesses as they try to improve on the weaknesses over time. While most people may look at them like flawless beings, people at the top have realized their weaknesses, but they

have deliberately chosen to not dwell on it. Early in your career, for instance, your boss may seem to be flawless in everything, but if you listened to them on a personal level, you would understand that everyone has weaknesses. It is only a matter of how you treat your weaknesses. It can control you, but you have the potential to control it.

Realize that you cannot be competent at everything. Once you realize this, you focus more on your strength to become more productive and happier. You will cease engaging in activities that you know you may not impact much and you will stay away from frustration. Most importantly, realize that strength is not only something you are good at but something that makes you feels strong as well. Therefore, embrace your fortes and steer clear of your weaknesses.

Focus on The Long-Term

While it is good to take your journey step by step, it is also good to focus on the bigger picture. A top secret for the top 1 percent achievers is delaying their gratification until they have gotten to the top. While the other 99 percent satisfies their short-term cravings, the top 1 percent always keeps their eyes on the grand prize. Neither efforts nor courage are enough without a long-time prize that you wait. For without the long-term vision, your energy often is directed to the less important functions. Even as you set minor goals and milestones in life, it is good to picture where you want to get.

Focus on Finding Solutions to Your Challenges

Relentless Mental Toughness and Optimism

They key accomplishing most of your life's crucial goals is constantly finding solutions to your challenges. There are two different ways, however, in which we approach problems in life. While most of the people have a problem-based approach and keep wondering why the problem emerged, the top 1 percent of people are solution oriented; hence they focus on identifying possible solutions. While the problem-oriented approach helps us to avoid similar problems in the future, we should first focus on finding a solution for the challenge at hand and deal with the cause later.

The problem-focused approach often has negative influences on a person's motivation. Having this mindset helps you live your everyday life purposefully. Whenever we know we are to face a challenging task or have an activity-filled day ahead, we can decide to approach such situations from a positive or a negative viewpoint.

Understand that how well you find solutions to your challenges determines how you move past the various hurdles that life may present. It sets you apart from the crowd that may decide to just sit around in the excuse of a challenge that they are facing.

Chapter 10:
How to Actually Break Bad Habits

Do you struggle with too much TV or social media while you shouldn't be engaged with either? Or eating too many burgers and sodas while you know the truth- that these have detrimental impacts on your health? Bad habits may seemingly be harmless activities or indecisions that are easy to overlook. Any activity qualifies to be called a habit when individuals cannot stop doing them. They develop over time to be fully integrated within our system that we cannot stay without doing it. To us, it even feels normal even if some voice in our head may tell us that what we are doing is probably not good for us. Sometimes, we feel too lazy and become too ignorant to find out the detrimental impacts of the habit in our lives.

But do not be deceived. Bad habits can potentially harm your entire life and prevent you from realizing your optimal purpose. Maybe, you have a habit that you struggle getting rid of. The truth of the matter is that you still have the power to fix your bad habits no matter how much they are engrained into our systems. Even though it is not easy, it is definitely possible. It is up to you to confront and attack that character before it destroys you. It is never too late to take a reverse gear and start living a more purposeful and healthier life.

Every change begins with an understanding of the system. You embark on the journey to change your habits by first gaining an understanding of how habits work. Research has it that every habit has a system through which it develops and becomes commonplace in our lives that we do them without resistance and without thinking. Typically, habitual behaviors go unnoticed because one does not need to analyze what they are about to do. Also, they are hard to break because of the behavioral patterns that become completely imprinted.

All habits work in a system of cues and rewards. The cue is also referred to as the trigger that induces the brain to get into the thing it does in a routine form. There are internal cues which are based on your emotional state and external cues which occurs when you see something, and it reminds you that you should be doing a certain thing. Further, the routine is now the action that we do as a habit; that which your mind actually allows you to take. Finally, the reward is typically what we get from performing the routine. Each habit has a reward which signals our brain that we actually need to take action. Therefore, the process of breaking a bad habit has all to do with studying the cues and rewards and knowing how to best go around them. The following is an easy way of breaking a bad habit:

First is to eliminate the cue, which works especially if the cue does not have to be seen every day. For instance, if your cue is meeting friends in a pub, and then you end up taking alcoholic drinks (routine) and get the fulfilling feeling that alcohol gives you (reward), you should seek to block the cue by choosing a different meeting spot. While alcoholic drinks are often taken for pleasure and relaxation, you may realize that consuming it every other day inhibits your thinking and derails you in your work. Therefore, you have to take the first step of blocking the cue.

However, if the cue cannot be avoided, such as having a mobile phone and Wi-Fi which sends the signal to your mind that you actually need to check your social media accounts, you should take the step of making the routine difficult. Use the concept of the 20-percent rule to manage your activation energy. This concept plays around with your mind since it is often so hard to start trying harder for something that you are used to having so easily. For instance, to reduce the amount of time you spend on social media, you can disable the functioning of social media apps in your mobile devices and leave your social media accounts deactivated. The effort of having to reactivate your accounts when you want to access social media will keep you off from them.

The other step you can take to dismantle the system of a habit is by making the reward unsatisfying. This is probably tricky to do, but it is definitely possible. It refers to the concept of identifying something that gives you a higher level of satisfaction or reward than the bad habit does, yet with less dangerous effects on you. Consider this. It is the feeling of sweetness that one has after eating an ice-cream which makes them crave for it. But once you identify something different, say milk, which gives you a good feeling yet you know it is more beneficial to your health, you will be able to override the seemingly pleasant feeling you have from taking ice-cream. More so, the following are the tips you should consider to make a change in your habits:

If behavior can be controlled, then it is a habit. It is contrasted with addiction, which is very hard to stop. With strong willpower, one is able to subdue the bad habits.

Pre-Commit to Change

Change can be scary. In a way, we all enjoy the comfort and stability associated with sameness. We only realize its effects once this has taken us down a road of complacency, and we become irrelevant. First, understand that change is a must, and if you do not initiate it, change will overwhelm. You will realize when it is too late down the road that you actually needed to change to achieve a certain goal. Then, your life will be a mess.

Conversely, pre-committing to change ensures that you are ready to handle the developing new you. You are ready to do what it takes to achieve the desired you. To break off the bad habit that is inherent in your system, be honest with yourself to understand that you really need change, and you will be ready to embrace it. If you have pre-committed yourself, for instance, to stop being on social media too much, you should uninstall the applications on all your devices. Also, if you have decided to stop sitting a lot without exercising, you should identify a way, for instance, walking a manageable distance that you used to drive home.

Assign Yourself a Challenge, Say 30-Day Challenge.

Have you ever promised yourself to stick to a personal goal, but then your intention fell ineffective a few days later? I suppose yes.

There is still hope for you. A 30-day challenge can help you out. It is an excellent strategy that has been used successfully to develop good new habits or break old bad ones. This challenge is as specific and timely as possible; hence it is measurable and easy to stick with. Rather than telling your mind that you do not have to stay online for five hours a day for the rest of your life, make it a challenge to have at most, say, 20 minutes on social media per day for thirty days.

Whenever you want to break an old habit, a spark of excitement may keep you going. You will even acquire the tools needed for you to forego that habit. Say, a skipping rope that will help you exercise. However, you are only excited for the first few days until you realize that you were not actually getting rewarded for the overwhelming long-term goal that you set. If you do not want to give up shortly after starting, embark on the 30-day challenge. You may be surprised that your challenge will form into a habit. If it becomes a new habit, make sure to add another habit onto it to prevent it from becoming boring. Experts have it that developing about 12 challenges in a year is pretty simple and manageable.

Attach a Tangible Reason to Your Desired Change

'Why you are seeking a change' is a question that may have to ask yourself before you even plan on how you are to change. Is it that you want more money? Is it that you want to achieve a life goal and you have identified a habit that may be hindering you? Is it that you want to live a healthy lifestyle and your habits such as eating unhealthy and lack of exercise hinder you?

What motivates you in acquiring the desired change is attaching a goal to it. Realize that you may never progress if your habit still holds you down. Every successful person had to make a choice at some point that they needed to make every day count in their journey to achieving their goals. Even the world's most renowned athletes knew that to be globally celebrated of their success they had to practice physical and mental exercises every day. You wouldn't find such a person stuck on the internet for five hours a day. Also, you wouldn't find them taking junks for the better part of the day. Therefore, attaching change to a goal is far much better than blindly going about it.

Start Small

Whenever you realize that you are constantly struggling to achieve your goals, one of the contributing factors is that your mind has it that the goals are too big to accomplish.

We often talk of the much-needed change but do not realize that it all boils down to an individual to effect the change. We may accept the value that change will add to our lives, but we do not actually strategize to know the way to get there. For instance, it is unreasonable for an ice-cream lover to think that they would shut down their bad habit all at once. It happens through the way of small steps to get you there. A person who does not read and has realized that to be knowledgeable and achieve their goals in life they have to start reading cannot embark on reading 3 books in a month. Even people who are not used to the gym do not go lifting the heavyweights. You can always start as small as it may seem, even reading just 5 pages a day. You will realize eventually that you increase the time you set aside for reading, and you begin to make it there. They begin small, and eventually, they build the momentum that is needed to adapt to the new lifestyle.

Track Change:
One of the best success driving habits is tracking down and measuring your success. You definitely need to measure and track down the progress you are making regarding your habits. A habit tracker is basically a to-do list of the items you are trying to stop or embrace. You tick off or make a record of what you are trying to measure.

Relentless Mental Toughness and Optimism

A tracker helps you to realize where you need some new mechanism of affecting your change. It helps to show the activities that give you the best results. It also motivates you to realize that the baby steps you are making are actually adding up to some good change. More so, it helps to keep you focused on avoiding breaking the chain. Most people fail to achieve the desired change because they forget why they started and the reward they looked forward to getting. Once you do not track and measure, you are most likely to focus on your failures and see the negative side of things. You will most probably focus on the reward you are foregoing more than the goal you are focused towards.

It is important to track the results from each step, say a daily entry of the progress. If you are embarking on reading books, record the number of pages that you read each day. You will realize that you have created a pattern in a few weeks. A tracker can help you look back and take pride in the progress of the work you have managed in the past. It also strengthens the momentum by having to activate the new task daily, and eventually, your mind never feels like the task is uncommon.

Change Your Identity
We already have it that every change begins from the mind. You tell your mind what to believe in and what not to believe in. We identify with what we tell our minds we are. Therefore, one of the essential steps of breaking a bad habit is changing our identity. We no longer

identify ourselves as say, smokers or obese. We break that identity in our minds. Whenever you are performing a habit, there is a voice in your mind which tells you that you identify with the habit. Also, when we want to change a habit, we are literally losing a part of us. Therefore, we should cease to identify ourselves with action and set our minds free. For instance, you no longer call yourself lazy. Rather, you consider yourself a person who has unproductive habits. Also, try to instill positive identities in your mind. For instance, start calling yourself a strong and healthy person before you embark on the gym training and healthy feeding. Start associating yourself with wisdom before you start reading books to become more knowledgeable.

Start Changing Your Bad Habits Today.

Let's recap. A habit forms through a pattern of behavior that becomes innately part of our daily lives. A habit that forms in us can be either good or bad. It begins with a mental trigger that develops a routine of action and leads to a reward. Habits are also hard to stop, but they can definitely be stopped.

All you have to do is apply the above techniques and move away from procrastination. Start today because tomorrow comes and you will have already made the first baby step. Procrastination is a delay habit that can destroy your life purposes. When you start today and avoid taking tasks to tomorrow while you have the potential to do it today, you are able to do other things without the guilt of having pending issues. Also, it takes you a step closer to your end goal.

Relentless Mental Toughness and Optimism

Mind every single choice you make no matter how small it may be. We often make minor decisions that may unknowingly change our course. In fact, this takes us back to the system through which a habit form. Any choice has the potential of getting us closer to where we want to be or getting us off our course. Each of them starts with a decision that we consciously or unconsciously make. Therefore, we should be mindful of every decision that we take along our way every day.

Chapter 11:
The Difference between Winners and Losers

Human beings are intrinsically driven towards competition. It is our ultimate source of pride. Contemporary society especially conditions us to be competitive. In every field of our lives, those who make it are those who possess the winning attitude and characteristics. Also, society has made being a winner the symbol of success. It neither tolerates failure nor does it make it an option. We all compete for various resources in life. And then, there are winners, and there are losers. The truth of the matter is that we all have the potential to become winners. The top achievers are aggressive people who put in work and dedicate all their energy into becoming successful. Who wouldn't admire to lead a happy and successful life? Who wouldn't want to get rich and travel the world and achieve their ultimate satisfaction levels? If you are fed up with losing or you simply want to win more, you have to put in the work. You have to differentiate between what makes a loser and what makes a winner.

As a starter, what you need to know is that a winner is always part of the answer and a loser is always part of the problem. You contribute towards the end of the course that you take. You want to be a winner;

you are going to have to contribute immensely towards that. Also, being a loser, you knowingly and unknowingly contribute to becoming one.

The following is a checklist of differences between winners and losers. It shows the things that winners do and do not do.

Do Not Crumble Under Pressure:
In all honesty, life presents its own pressures in ways we cannot prevent at times. It all depends on how we handle that pressure and make it work for our own good. Having had a taste of both sides, I can tell you with confidence that top achievers do not crumble under pressure, but the losers are easily crushed by pressure. Even your most valuable skills do no matter if you cannot perform when you are required to perform the best during competitive pressure. Experts argue that how we perform under pressure is a reflection of our mental capacity to respond to the situation. It is our human response to stress that allows us to meet the demands of the pressuring moment that differentiates between winners and losers.

Simply stated, winners approach pressure in a challenge state while losers approach pressure in a threat state. Most often, the threat state blocks our ability to perform efficiently and focus on the positive side. The challenged state, on the other side, activates the part of our brain that is able to calm our nerves down and take an accurate and efficient decision. Take a look back at a single time when you failed in something. Say, for instance, an interview. You may realize that you actually felt worried about the situation and that you were highly uncertain prior to the situation. Most often, the fear to fail makes us overthink the situation, and it even hinders us from presenting our best selves. An interview, in this case, is considered one of the high-pressure situations where every word you say and every move you make is being observed by your potential boss. They study you to see if you are a good match for the values and needs of their company. A simple error makes you lose your chance for the job even if you have the skills it takes. In these situations, the confident candidate who handles the situation articulately acquires the job while others fail.

Now that we know that how you handle pressure determines whether you fail or you win, it is paramount that you break the habit of overthinking situations and performing poorly, and adopt the "never bowing in to pressure" attitude. When you enter a high-pressure situation, activate your ability to focus on the task. Do not waste your time and energy thinking about how you'll perform. When you become too anxious about the pressure you are facing, you are much more likely to perform in a way that is contrary to your goals and strategies. The good news is that we can all train our minds to see the positive side of the challenge and successfully pursue it.

Do Not Have A Negative Self-Image.
Self-image is basically the mental picture we have of ourselves in mind. It is about who you perceive yourself to be, and it stems from

Relentless Mental Toughness and Optimism

the ideas and beliefs we have about ourselves. The image you have about yourself influences how you carry yourself around every day. How you feel and think is tied down to your self-image. Interestingly, it also influences how other people see you because it reflects in your body language and general demeanor. The thing is, the winners have a positive self-image, and the losers have a negative self-image. Winners are never stopped by how others think about them, the kind of social status they have, or even the events in the past that might have tampered with their self-esteem, including peers that might have teased them about being different in a certain way or being ugly or being a weakling. Winners rise above such things and train their mind to think the best about themselves.

Your mental state is in peril if you are full of negative self-image. Just because in your lineage no one ever excelled in mathematics, you start thinking you were just born that way. Just because no one ever became an athlete, you start thinking it is a family thing, and you can never win in athletics. You let such thoughts hinder you from pursuing the path that may have brought you success in the long-run. You spend your entire life believing that you cannot make it and you give excuses about your abilities not being enough. You automatically anticipate the worst, and you often blame yourself if you mess up once. Failure becomes your biggest enemy because you think you have to be perfect. You magnify the negative parts of a situation and dismiss the positive sides since you have a negative self-image which becomes the basis of your thoughts and actions. Then at the final end, you become a loser.

Be like the winners. Believe that you can actually make it. We were all created equal, just that our paths are different. However, we can all be successful in our unique way. Start looking at yourself as someone worthy of the good things in life. That mindset is enough to take you through your journey of being successful.

Do Not Play to Lose

The biggest secret of personal success is to identify your calling and play to it. The great question for success is, whatsoever, do you have the winning or the losing mindset. One thing that is common among the most renowned achievers is that they never play to lose. They never let the fact that they could lose get in their way.

It is one thing to establish your zone of genius, and it is another to operate in it. Things are not always easy. Believing that you have the capability to achieve is easy to say but not to achieve. One day you are on top of the world, and on another day, you are overwhelmed by a wave of doubt in your abilities. The fear of failure and not having what it takes may make us lead our lives half-heartedly. However, the most successful people do not entertain such thoughts. They never let such factors undermine their motivation to perform. They have their mind focused on the grand prize they are to realize from working hard and smart.

Relentless Mental Toughness and Optimism

It is the motivational focus in life that influences how we approach life's demands. Promotion-focused people are always eager to play and win. They see their goals and paths as a way of advancing. Further, they focus on the rewards they get when they achieve their goals. Such people play to win because to them, the worst thing they know about is a chance not taken to advance. Also, they work quickly since they want to get things done as opposed to lazing around. Further, they focus on the long-term benefit that they sacrifice the short-term pleasure and step onto the time-limited painful step.

Importantly also, winners do not engage in stuff that requires them to be different from the person they believe they are. They have to ask themselves if what they are doing requires them to change their personality. They have to know if it is right for them, and they have to know if it is sustainable. Further, they always do due diligence since they believe the reality, they owe themselves is that it is going to work out. Most importantly, the winners know that their inner life determines their outer circle. They know that it is all in mind to concentrate on failure or success.

Therefore, do it like a winner and always play to win.

Are Always Committed

Most people claim to have an understanding of the importance of setting goals in their lives to get to that better life that they desire. But in the actual fact, most of these people have no goals for themselves.

This is particularly true for people who are not involved in some sort of commercial undertaking that endorses the setting of goals. Even more surprising, science has it that above 90 percent of the people who set goals do not achieve them. We have all at some points in our lives set goals that have not been achieved. We experience a setback, and it wears down our willingness to stay committed to the goal. Considering that most people who set goals often target the easily achievable goals, it is surprising that other people are able to accomplish highly in their lives.

But the reason why successful people become more successful while the losers deteriorate further into the losing end is clear. They are passionate about their goals, and they stay committed to the end. Whenever obstacles pop up in their lives, they are totally sold out to reaching their goal, and they never lose sight of it. When it comes to goals, the winners realize the significance of commitment. The difference between simply desiring something and being committed to achieving it is also clear. When you are committed, you do not entertain excuses-you are only focused on results. Commitment influences how you think and act. You always try harder and do not consider quitting an option.

Be like the winners; pursue your goals relentlessly despite what may come along. Take a quick moment, and check into yourself. If you are not really committed to achieving your goal, it doesn't matter how appealing or challenging it is-you are just not going to achieve it.

Relentless Mental Toughness and Optimism

To stay committed to your goal, lean on a trusted coach, avoid multitasking, and track your progress. It doesn't matter how much talented you are, or you believe you are rather, seeking expert guidance makes a big impact in achieving your goals. The winners surround themselves with winners, those who will support their journey. Also, they are patient and take one thing at a time, since cooking from too many pots at a go can be detrimental to their success. Handling too many tasks may diminish your commitment, and make you split your focus, and, therefore, lower the quality of your work. If a number of them fail, you may spend too much time correcting others, and this reduces your commitment levels. Typically, commitment gives you a footprint of how to handle things when times get tough. Commit today and enjoy being a winner tomorrow!

Do Not Dream Small.

One of the most popular sayings that we consider cliché is "aim for the sun and land at the moon." Now, we know that the sun stands at a much higher altitude than the moon. A right mindset and necessary actions can definitely push you to reach the moon if not the sun. The moon, after all, is a high position that can shine down light to everyone else. Typically, the good thing about dreaming big is that even if you fall short you will still have gained a lot. We only limit ourselves, yet the sky is the limit. What successful people do not do is that they do not limit themselves. They trust their ability to achieve anything. They look up to other successful people and know that if someone else, with the same 24 hours in a day has achieved, they can also achieve.

Never let the position you are at today hinder you from deciding where you are headed. You might be in a hopeless position in your career, for instance, such that this dampens your ambition in life. Your mind may tell you to be conservative about your dreams to have a smaller blow should your dream fall short. While setting big goals does not exactly mean you'll achieve them, failure to set them definitely means that you have nothing to achieve. Winners maximize on the time they have to gain the possible positive experiences. Truth be told; life has no rehearsal, and life is short! Do not settle for mediocrity. Understand that big things do come true when one has the courage to pursue them.

Imagine someone whose dream is to be the next top athlete. Such a high goal pushes you to heights you may not reach otherwise. They require a lot of hard work and achievement. You may not make it there but definitely a lot of good will come out of it. While there are plenty lots of benefits from leaving an ordinary life where complacency is entertained, and compliance is not executed, there is nothing quite like being a dreamer and having wild visions of a life you aspire to leave.

Winners envision success well enough that they are able to feel it since as the universe has it; whatever we can imagine we can become.

Relentless Mental Toughness and Optimism

Losers never want to imagine goals that may disrupt their common life. Be a winner, and set yourself aside from the losers.

Chapter 12:
Guaranteed Strategies to Build Mental Toughness

With all said, it all boils down to mental toughness. It has been described as the ability to bounce back from failure and respond articulately to adversity and to work relentlessly toward your life's purpose. In other words, it is the inherent state of mind which propels people to keeping toward the future they desire.

Now, intellectual strength shapes the foundation for success in the long run. People who have made it in life are associated with a particular personality trait that makes them persevere and remain passionate about their long-term goals. For instance, mentally-tough people are known for withstanding temptation. They also overcome fear and go on to do what they need to do. What they have deliberated as valuable to their life purpose, the remarkable top achievers consistently and uninterruptedly keep doing it. These qualities require mental toughness. It is no coincidence, therefore, that those are the qualities of the successful people.

To develop mental toughness and consequently become more successful, here are the things you need to consider and do:

Relentless Mental Toughness and Optimism

Have a Mindset of Total Control?

Believing that you are in control of your life to be able to own up to your successes and failures responsible is among the crucial mind-strengthening habits. Be responsible for your own self and nothing will move you out of focus. You won't waste energy worrying about what might or might not happen to you. Instead, you will invest in making things happen. Direct your energy into realizing your end goal and reaping the fruits of success.

While most of us tend to believe that luck will play out to get us what we need in life, the mentally tough people like to be responsible for their own life. They identify what works best for them and where they are talented in. As long as they have made the first step, they believe that nothing is unachievable. Such people do not listen to the noise of the world surrounding them discouraging them from losing the sight of their vision or from losing balance over their lives.

However, the difference between being in total control and actually dwelling on things that do not align with your destiny is clear.

Do Not Dwell on Things You Do Not Have the Ability to Impact

There is so much obscurity in the concept of having control over one's life that tends to make us fail in achieving it. There are factors that come in shaping us as individuals and also shaping our future. Some of these are completely out of your control. Trying to control them to bend to your desires will only frustrate you and diminish your energy.

It takes a lot of courage to admit that that's the reality we live in, and there's no way around it. Once you realize that there are certain things beyond your control in a life that is where you draw the line.

We tend to spend too much time worrying about the affairs that are totally out of our capability. Obviously, concentrating what goes around in the world has profound effects on our lives. It triggers our emotional responses to our lives. We start doubting our abilities to achieve. We start seeing ourselves as less talented. But that is all in our minds. How we respond to things that are beyond us is entirely in our minds. We have the ability to control ourselves and nothing else.

The mentally tough people always take time to breathe and relax whenever they encounter situations beyond their control.

Consider the Past as Valuable Training and Nothing More

For a majority of people, they understand that dwelling on past events, especially failure and mistakes, is much likely to ruin our present and our future by holding us back from going forth. However, most of us are tied down by allowing thoughts about our past to dominate our minds.

Yet, one of the most powerful ingredients of the successful people is taking time to analyze what they should take from the past and what should not bother them. To them, the past can only be used to train them to become better versions of themselves but not to hinder them from approaching the present and future with confidence. We waste our worthy time feeling sorry for ourselves for things that happened long ago. But the truth is we all have the capacity to become mentally stronger by letting the past go and taking only the useful lessons with us. As mentioned earlier, being retrospective allows you to analyze the past and know what you picked from a situation and that can be applied in the future. This also applies when approaching challenges in life. Having a solution-based approach to problems often helps you focus on the present and the future rather than past experiences. It allows you to see the challenge as an opportunity to learn something you did not know.

You become stronger by having many lessons and values you can apply in life.

Celebrate Another Person's Success

The society has become so cruel that the shining of another person is considered as a diminishing of another person's light. People consider success as a zero-sum game which when one gains something it automatically makes another person lose that thing.

But that is not how a mentally tough person is. They know that resentment will only add them mental baggage which will consequently reduce their productiveness in other areas. They also understand that resentment does not stop other people from shining. Therefore, once a person they know wins at something, they are happy for them. If a friend won a tough interview, they are happy for them. In fact, they draw closer to have a taste of what success feels like and to gain the tactics that such people employed.

Remember that another person's win does not reduce your chances to win. You should help them celebrate and take the motivation that such a win give. In fact, once of cliché sayings that we should consider very relevant in our lives is that birds of a feather flock together. Associate with people who have big winnings. Celebrate success wherever you find it, and you will condition your mind on having more of such success in your life.

More so, mentally tough people do not criticize others because they know that everyone has something to offer. They refrain from passing unfair judgment because they need not need pull others down to feel good about themselves. They understand that everyone has their path in life and they celebrate the unique talents of others.

Cease to Complain

We have heard time and over again that we attract what we always think. Your words and thoughts have power over you. If you are always complaining, then you have a negative attitude towards life, and this weighs you down. Most people have the tendency of complaining over even the pettiest things including traffic delays, the weather and a queue at the store. They think that complaining will make them feel better, but they fail to understand the power that complaining has over their lives.

Relentless Mental Toughness and Optimism

The mentally tough people do not waste time complaining. They know the inner peace that comes from not complaining. They allow others to be and become generally happier. This improves their clarity of mind, and they are able to go about their daily lives better. Be like the mentally tough. Do not talk about the situation that is wrong. Instead, concentrate on how you can make your life better. Also, do not listen to other people complain to you. Be kind and help them improve by showing them the limitations of complaining.

Focus on Impressing Only Yourself

Among the greatest accomplishments in life is the ability to be yourself when the world is constantly trying to mold you into a different form. There is a lot of pressure from the society which influences how we live and interact with others. This has the potential to make you lose yourself and want to live your life by the standards set by others. There is a chance that you follow what others want you to be or remain true to your purpose. Realize that successful people do not compare themselves with others since they know that this is a limiting aspect in their lives. They do not waste their time trying to wonder whether or not they measure up. Instead, they funnel that energy into creating a better version of themselves.

If you want to realize your ultimate purpose, it all starts with being yourself and doing what makes you happy. You should know what is right to do and what not to do. You should know yourself and your limits, and then live a more rewarding life without being pushed from side to side. Even when you want to focus on helping others and celebrating another people's success, you have to start by being yourself and pleasing yourself. When you work to impress others, and it turns out that they do not appreciate your efforts, you become frustrated, and you keep trying to conform to their values to please them. Once they invalidate something, you try to look for one that they will definitely acknowledge. At the end of the day, what you are doing does not add value to your personal being. You cannot have control over what you say, do, wear, eat or even work. It is easy to spend your entire life wasting your energy on things that will never lead you to your ultimate life's purpose. We are all different in our special way and it is only by embracing our uniqueness that we are able to succeed in our own unique way. The world's best athlete might not have been able to reach their success if they wanted to please the world's best entrepreneur, who was busy pursuing their goal.

Count Your Blessings
Take a moment every day to appreciate what you have. This will keep you from worrying about what you do not have and will most definitely make you happier. You will also stop comparing yourself with others over what they have that you do not.

Be grateful every time for what you have, as you await what you desire. When you keep appreciating what you have every day, you will be motivated to work harder and achieve more. It is not always about making a huge achievement at once. It is also about the little things that count. Even single drops of water can fill a tank over a long time. Appreciating what you have will also align your energy into being happy and positive always. You will find out that there's a lot to be grateful about. Feeling good about you is a powerful mental recharge.

Furthermore, counting your blessings will make you go through tough times more easily. We all encounter difficult times in our lives, and it feels like we are the worst-case scenario. If all you chose to see is the problem of the moment, how do you expect better times? How do you expect to be happy? You have to deliberately seek to find at least one thing you can feel blessed about no matter what your day entails. Before you realize it, your list of blessings will grow and you will grow along with it. Conversely, focusing only on what you have not achieved fills your spirit with sadness. Therefore, you should focus on your blessings to radiate your life.

Do Not Wait for An Apology to Forgive

One of the toughest things in the world to do is to forgive someone who has caused you pain and suffering. Most probably, we have all been in situations that called for forgiveness-asking for it and giving it. Daily interactions with fellow humans are difficult since we all have conflicting ideas, interests, and wants. We are by default, therefore, bound to have conflicts, misunderstandings, strain, and division. We find it hard to forgive because we are all, by nature, self-centered. We want anyone who wounds us to accept fault for what they did, ask for forgiveness, and even so, we still want to make them feel indebted to us.

Mentally tough people, however, know how that forgiveness is a brave action that they forgive even people who never apologize. Negative occurrences are from the past mess with your happiness today, and they take from you so much energy. Abhorrence and rage are just parasites in your life that you had better get rid of. The negative emotion attached to anger triggers a response in you that has devastating impacts on your health and wellbeing. Forgiveness reduces blood pressure, eliminates anxiety, and improves our sleep quality. Consequently, this improves our decision making, and our lives become more high quality. Forgiveness qualifies as an attribute for the strong. Be a strong person and forgive.

Some of the things that you ought to understand to help you in forgiving people are that imperfection is part of human nature, forgiveness improves your life even if not theirs, it is not in your place to judge people and also there is karma to repay people for their actions. Move on with your life and leave what already happened in the past.

Finally, Be Mindful of How You Regard the Word "Quit"
We all feel like throwing in the towel from time to time. No matter how prepared you are for a journey in life, things happen and throw us in a dilemma as we wonder whether or not quitting is the right choice.

Relentless Mental Toughness and Optimism

People quit for different reasons, including running projects that end up as a mere mess or at times because they feel like they are safer not pushing forward.

However, you should always consider some things when you want to quit: What is making you quit? You find that most of the time we feel like quitting because of the negative energy we have fed our minds with. Once you understand why you really want to quit, consider if it a good reason, what perseverance would bring to you, if you are likely to regret the action, and most importantly, why you started what you are about to quit in the first place. Once you train yourself to take these steps, you will go harder about your goals, and you will hardly quit anything. You will be like the Navy SEALS or the marathoners. They hardly quit once they are set out on a mission or a competition. We all celebrate their success eventually, and they lead a fulfilled life.

Now we know the things that separate those who are good from those who are great. We understand why mental toughness is such a huge factor that it overrides the potential of talent. We understand that building our capacities to handle adversity is so much about removing the harmful habits that consume our energy and hinder us from achieving our purpose in life. Now, it is time to go out there to create goals and make our dreams happen.

Marcus J. Clark

Conclusion

In conclusion, this guide describes the concept of mental toughness, its relevance in our lives, and how we can develop mental toughness. Mental toughness is a popular concept yet which only a few understood. For a long time in history, mental toughness has been thought of as a thing for the sports people or the Navy SEALs. Recently, however, it has become relevant in various fields as researchers and coaches attempt to offer people the crucial tactics that these most successful people have in common, and that has helped them to achieve this success. This guide takes us through what it means to refrain from putting about our limitations in mind. It directs us how to be as relentless about our goals as ever. It shows us how to persevere and never think of the word "quit" as an option in our journey to achieving our goals. It differentiates between winners and losers to help us see what makes two people, gifted uniquely but on the same playing field achieve different results, whereby one succeeds and one fails. It shows us how we can develop daily success habits and also how we can break from bad habits and create good habits. It gives us techniques from the Navy SEALs that we can embrace to become

Relentless Mental Toughness and Optimism

mentally tough and pull through every situation that tries to beat us down in life.

The reason why the Navy SEALs is the most admired army is that among other armed forces, the SEALs undergo the toughest training, and they also undertake the most dangerous missions. It is interesting how these troops carry out their dangerous missions to completion with all the challenges that they face. They never quit. They focus on the end of the mission and not the mistakes or misfortunes that have happened in the past. They are ever prepared to face challenges, and even when the unexpected occurs, they do not stop to wonder whose fault it was that the misfortune befell them. It is all about their mindset. They have a positive mindset which sees challenges as opportunities from which they can learn. Also, they are able to approach challenges from a solution-based perspective and not as a threat. They employ various principles to know how to best handle a situation. Most importantly, the SEALs funnel their energy towards their mission and focus on the prize at the final end. Another admired group is that of the marathoners. Research has it that almost all marathoners who begin a race keep at it to completion. They are able to rise above several hurdles that they face along the way because they focus on the bigger picture: the finish line. Essentially, therefore, this guide shows us how to enhance our performance with a simple mindset switch.

Marcus J. Clark

Among the points that the book emphasizes is that there are physical limits but none for the mind. Every time we are faced with a situation such as adversity, our performance is always influenced by our ability to balance between internal and external demands placed on us. We often emphasize on physical training or simply highlight our talent at something, but we ignore the mental training that is more paramount than anything else. Every other factor held constant during a contest, a person with the right mindset has a high chance of defeating one with the wrong mindset. We are human, and we are bound to experience critical points in life that make us want to quit our goals unless we feed our minds with success. Purpose, self-awareness, goals, visualizing success, team support, preparation, positive self-talk, focusing on progress, not perfection and celebrating the small winnings are some of the most ingredients prerequisites for success. We achieve this by showing our minds that this is the way to do it. Without a strong will power, we cannot manage these other tactics.

From the mind of a Navy SEAL part, we learn to never procrastinate, to think of discipline not as a punishment, to consider the 10 second rule when making decisions, to be ready to do what the 1 percent people will do that the 99 percent others will not, to consider the long-term, to make progress on ourselves and not dwell on competing against others, and to always maintain these habits in every undertaking that we engage in. Further, the daily habits that strengthen the minds include waking up early, making the bed, create an ideal daily

Relentless Mental Toughness and Optimism

routine for us, to exercise regularly, to eat healthy, to DE-clutter our living spaces and our lifestyles, to keep a journal, and to meditate and conduct mind focus exercises.

To develop an unbeatable mind as opposed to a fragile mind, we ought to learn to make decisions not suggestions, to always know that we can achieve more, to not dwell on failure since we know there are various ways of do things, to welcome pressure and excel in it, to work harder even when everyone else is quitting, to remain humble in tough situations, and to remain accountable of our ideas and results. An important concept also discussed is the 40 percent rule, in which we should know that whenever we think we are done, we are actually only 40 percent done hence keep on with the grind. To achieve the 40 percent rule, we should give things a chance to be easy as opposed to having a quick and negative response to situations, concede that what we want is not the best we can achieve, and stop seeing the suffering but the value in it.

Further, the significance of confidence cannot be underrated when it comes to developing mental toughness. We should develop the confidence to lead and stand out among the crowd. To start building our confidence, we should develop a sense of curiosity, talk positively to ourselves, start doing what we want to be confident in, exercise, learn how to dress and carry ourselves around better, and improve our knowledge at every chance that we have. Also, we are reminded that setting goals keep us tied to our purpose, and we should always recite a mantra that strengthens our willpower. Also, to face a challenge, we should simulate an exactly similar situation, break down the challenge step by step, focus on what lies right ahead of us before we move to the next step, raise the stakes, bounce back quickly from the unexpected, achieve emotional control and identify where we belong.

We are also advised to follow the mental training of the top 1 percent; it is the group of people that comprises of achievers and who do things that others find difficult to do. To belong to this group, we ought to prioritize, regularly review our goals, and identify a niche where we can create value, complement our knowledge with action, create our own system, network, understand our strengths and weaknesses, focus on the bigger picture, and focus on finding solutions to our challenges. Most importantly, the strategies we all need to build mental toughness include having the mindset of total control, not dwelling on things we do not have the ability to control, considering the past as a valuable training, celebrating other people's success, stopping to complain, focusing on impressing ourselves and not others, counting our blessings and forgiving even when someone has not asked for an apology.

If you find this book helpful in anyway a review to support my endeavors is much appreciated.

Relentless Mental Toughness and Optimism

Marcus J. Clark

www.ingramcontent.com/pod-product-compliance
Lightning Source LLC
Chambersburg PA
CBHW060455080526
44584CB00015B/1443